TURNING TO GOD

*Anglicans Talk about Sin, Grace,
and the Christian Life*

The Primate's Theological Commission
Anglican Church of Canada

resource
ABC Publishing
ANGLICAN BOOK CENTRE

ABC Publishing
Anglican Book Centre
600 Jarvis Street
Toronto, Ontario
Canada M4Y 2J6

Editorial: Joanne McWilliam, Greig Dunn
Educational Consultant: Walter Deller
Design: Saskia Rowley, Jane Thornton
Administration: Janet Thomas, Robert Maclennan

National Library of Canada Cataloguing in Publication Data
Main entry under title:

Turning to God : Anglicans talk about sin, grace, and the Christian life.

(Wrestling with God ; bk. 2)
ISBN 1-55126-344-0

1. Christian life—Anglican authors. 2. Anglican Communion—Doctrines. I. Anglican Church of Canada. Primate's Theological Commission. II. Series.

BX5615.A1T87 2002   230'.3   C2002-900025-4

TABLE OF CONTENTS

HOW THEN SHOULD WE LIVE?

CONTRIBUTORS

Robert Crouse

Walter Deller

Edith Humphrey

Laverne Jacobs

Hanna Kassis

Christopher Lind

Victoria Matthews

Joanne McWilliam

Michael Peers

David Reed

Eileen Scully

VICTORIA MATTHEWS

Since the publication of book one, *Longing for God*, the General Synod of the Anglican Church of Canada has met in Waterloo, Ontario, and the world has been shaken by the events of 11 September 2001. Both the threat of bankruptcy and the attacks on the World Trade Center and elsewhere have left us feeling vulnerable and uncertain. What better time could there be to consider "turning to God" and the topics of sin, grace, and the Christian life?

On the ecclesiastical stage, concern continues among some about orthodoxy and the limits of Anglican diversity. At General Synod a discussion about the blessing of same-sex unions was on the agenda, and we signed the Waterloo Declaration, thereby affirming full communion with the Evangelical Lutheran Church in Canada. The essays, reflections, and short comments in this book do not focus primarily upon the much discussed topics of the day, but invite Anglicans in Canada to consider the underlying theological realities. The attention of the Primate's Theological Commission was, and is, primarily directed to the importance of theology, and not to polity.

At General Synod in July 2001, the Primate's Theological Commission was asked to make a report. We engaged the Synod members in theological reflection, as well as showing a video of the Commission's work. The Commission was encouraged by the enthusiasm of Synod mem-

bers in discussing some of the Commissioners' statements on sin. It occurred to us that this frequently ignored theological subject may be due for a comeback. Certainly many of the hot topics of our day cannot be discussed adequately without a working understanding of sin, both personal and corporate.

As we reviewed this book, it became obvious that its pages reflect an acute almost omnipresent consciousness of the residential schools' history and resultant trauma. In considering this and other concerns, the volume is contextual. Nevertheless, an attempt has been made to identify and discuss the underlying theological questions that are much larger than Canada and our residential schools. The identification and challenge of the whole people of God is as present in the presentation of Jubilee described in Leviticus 25 as it is in the discussing of residential schools.

Last, but not least, is the question of Christian practice. In a world all aglow about spirituality and the almost endless meanings of the word, how Christians go about being disciples of Jesus Christ in their private, personal, and public life is tremendously important. Faithful living forms Christians and witnesses to the world. To that end, it is my hope that this volume will assist individuals and groups in both theological reflection and the life of grace.

INTRODUCTION

JOANNE McWILLIAM

In the first book in this series, *Longing for God*, members of the Primate's Theological Commission discussed the various ways God makes Godself known to us. We looked at revelation in itself, its relation to nature and culture, and the role of authority in Christian belief and practice.

While well aware that God is not revealed once for all, that revelation is an ongoing process both in individual lives and in history, the PTC decided that the next set of questions would cluster around How then do we turn to God? Here we look first at the human condition and the Christian condition, at the meaning of conversion, sin, and grace. And then, having turned initially to God (again an ongoing process), how are we nourished in the Christian life? By prayer (including mystical prayer and the sacraments). What is the relation between prayer and Christian living?

How, then, should we live? The group presents various understandings of what it means to live in the Spirit, followed by one member's view of what the Christian moral life entails. The question of discernment is vividly presented in a story of one member's struggle to reconcile Native Spirituality and Christianity. The view that Evangelism is concerned solely with the salvation of the individual is discussed and corrected. It is pointed out that there are different moral languages. One member emphasizes the Aboriginal view of nature as sacred. A piece on the very important "Jubilee initiative" follows. Contextual theology is described and three examples are given. There is an article on spiritual healing, and the book concludes with another group discussion: What is the role of Christian mission in today's church and world?

SIN AND GRACE

KEY QUESTIONS

Traditional Christian theology describes sin as turning away from God.

+ What forms does turning away from God take?
+ Is it intrinsic in our nature to turn away from God?
+ Although grace is a free gift of God that cannot be earned, the question arises to what extent our cooperation with God's grace is required for it to become effectual in and through us?
+ What connections are there between the wrongs done by individuals and the wrongs done by whole societies?
+ How are we enabled to turn back to God?

DIFFERENT VIEWS ON SIN

Commission members each wrote a short description of their understanding of sin. They read these aloud to one another; below are excerpts from the conversation that followed.

Robert Christian moral life consists in loving God above all, and loving all else only in that perspective. Accordingly, sin is a failure of love, whether as a perversion of self-love (as in pride, envy, wrath), a deficiency of love (as in sloth), or an inappropriate excess of love (as in avarice, gluttony, lust). Thus, sin is always a matter of will, never of circumstance or accident, and (whether we think of original sin or actual sins) it is always a matter of falling short of our high calling.

The grace of God's forgiveness, freely offered in Jesus Christ, both enlightens our minds to discern the good and liberates our wills to pursue it. That is, God's grace both strengthens and reorders our loves.

Eileen One Sunday I was present at the following "penitential rite":

Presider: "It's so awesome, we don't hear it often enough. I'm okay, you're okay."
People: "I'm okay, you're okay. God loves us just the way we are."

I had spent the previous day taking in the sights of a red-light district of the city where I live with its food banks and health clinics for the homeless, and in hearing the stories of survivors of residential schools. I was *not* okay. I was full of pain from carrying the weight of different realities all called "sin": a callous culture, the legacy of the schools, and my own defense mechanisms. Sin keeps poverty, violence, and suffering on the margins, and invisible to our consciousness. The affirmation, "God loves us just the way we are," rang empty. Worse, I feared that it perpetuates sin.

Joanne Eileen, I too am repelled by that so-called "penitential rite," but I can't help wondering what was behind it. Why did the congregation (or the presider) so badly need reassurance? Had the people of the congregation been scolded so often that they were aware only of sin, not of salvation?

Laverne One aspect of sin is the placing of oneself or one's own community above another, whether that other be the Creator, another person, or another people. Sin devalues the other. This self-centeredness leads to a kind of mission that sees others as less than ourselves, others (but not ourselves) as in need of salvation and civilization. It leads to colonialism, and it fostered the residential school system.

In the current climate of litigation it has led my diocese to emphasize a legal defence that identifies ministry with "saving the church." This is a "circling the wagons" policy that has enabled one diocese to deny any moral responsibility for its role in the Mohawk Institute and to dissociate itself from the national church. This position causes alienation, pain, and a sense of betrayal among the Native community.

Joanne We are created with an openness to the transcendent. **St. Augustine** reminds us that "our hearts are restless until they rest in [God]." Our frequent failures can lead us to think that sin is "natural," but sin is not part of human nature. Augustine also says, "The vice of the soul is not its nature, but contrary to its nature." This becomes obvious when we assert both that Christ was fully human and yet sinless.

God calls us all and offers grace sufficient for us to choose to turn away from ourselves and towards God. God does not coerce; we can ignore the call and refuse the offered grace. Would it have been better if we had been created unable to sin, formed so that we were compelled to fix our wills on God? No. A person who could not turn away from God could not turn towards God.

These remarks have been predicated of persons, but they also apply to societies. A society that turns its back on the homeless, the sick, children, and old people is a sinful society. We — its members — may be complicit in these evils.

David But, Joanne, in saying that sin is not part of human nature, are you taking it seriously enough? Your suggestion that we are able to turn to God sounds almost **Pelagian**. It suggests that

AUGUSTINE (354–430) was bishop of the North African city of Hippo Regius. He is counted as one of the "doctors" (i.e., teachers) of the church. His thought, particularly his theology of original sin and grace, has been especially influential in the Western church.

PELAGIUS was an ascetical leader of the late fourth and early fifth century who was accused by Augustine of teaching that we can save ourselves without the help of divine grace. This was not what Pelagius taught, but this misinterpretation has been associated with his name ever since. Pelagius believed in the necessity of divine grace, but he understood it differently than did Augustine. For Augustine, grace was primarily a mysterious internal movement of the soul; he rarely applied the term to externals. Pelagius, while not denying the interior workings of grace, also saw external events and realities as graces: for example, divine creation, the incarnation of the Word, the existence of the church and sacraments. Pelagius thought that Augustine's maxim, "Love God and do what you will," encouraged moral laziness, and that his preoccupation with sin did not sufficiently recognize the saving work of Christ.

to sin or not to sin is solely an act of our human wills.

Joanne No, it's not Pelagian; our turning to God *follows* God's gift of grace.

Eileen Your suggestion that we may be complicit in societal sin takes us back to the residential schools question. How are we complicit with something when we had no part in making the decisions that created it?

David Sin is like a near-fatal accident. By the time you realize you could have been killed, you are safe. This means, first of all, that sin is not strictly a *moral* term, something a culture calls wrong or "bad." It is a *theological* term describing a relationship between God and humanity.

Sin is also a *Christian* term that has meaning only in the context of the person and saving work of Jesus. I can feel restless, unfulfilled, enslaved, even guilty, but I cannot know sin until I encounter Jesus, who reveals my deep alienation from God, and who offers a new way of living. Sin is a situation that I am helpless to remedy.

Here lies the mystery of grace, grace that has been working behind the scene, through law and conscience, until Christ is revealed by the Spirit. He exposes our weakness and accomplishes God's saving power.

A confused world may consign sin to the law of nature and its consequences. But in Christ there is good news about sin: nature doesn't forgive, but God does.

Joanne David, I know that "sin" is a Judaeo-Christian word, but I am convinced that people of other religions are capable and conscious of going against the will of God, however they would describe it.

Edith Sin is such a dark "mystery." St. Paul nearly personifies sin as "reigning" over us, as something far greater than particular trespasses. Western Christendom typically sees sin as guilt, inherited from Adam. The Eastern Church, pleading God's justice, speaks of an inherited disordered nature in which we each follow Adam.

We re-enact the first sin daily and misuse God's gifts because we see God incorrectly and seek autonomy. In this dreary pattern we are both victims and perpetrators, experiencing separation within ourselves: from creation, from each other, and from God. Perhaps we are most brutalized by sins against the weak — the poor, the dispossessed, the unborn, the infirm, the old, and the young. For them and for us, the Holy One became the least.

Victoria What is sin? I am convinced of the truth of the teaching that each human being is created in the image and likeness of God, and that in and through sin, all have fallen short of the glory of God. Thus, sin is literally a shortcoming, a failure to be and do all one is called by God to be and do. Such sinfulness besets not only each individual, but also communities, nations, and the entire human population.

Sparked by a desire and decision to serve one-self and one's own self-interest, sin leads persons and peoples to give God far less than the fullest honour and glory.

Sin needs to be addressed from outside the sinful human race, and thus it is the perfect sacrifice of Jesus on the cross that offers us a new beginning. Thereafter, every Christian is invited to learn to walk with Christ, living the redeemed life even while still sinful.

Christopher Sin may be absent from modern language, but it's not absent from modern life. Sin is our tendency to separate ourselves from God in spite of our best efforts. Our modern age tends to focus all of our attention on individual actions and identity. However, our collective actions and identity are also subject to separation from God. We call this "social sin." Our families, organizations, and institutions have in-built tendencies to disease, disability, and dysfunction. Even our churches have both the capacity and the tendency to stray from truth, compassion, and justice.

Perhaps the most challenging social sins are those that occur where the best leaders of a generation have cooperated for the highest purposes, and still the results have included pain and sorrow, cruelty and injustice. Our ability to identify the sins of the past should not blind us to the sins of the present. We strive to achieve our highest ideals, but our successors will also find us wanting.

Hanna Like a delicious fruit stolen from someone else's orchard, sin is both sweet and forbidden. But whether we emphasize one or another of its opposing qualities, the troubling question remains, What is sin? In its simplest definition, sin is a violation of a divine law or commandment.

The author of Psalm 51 laments his association with sin from the day of his conception in his mother's womb. Is sin part of our biological makeup? Or is sin only a violation of a specific divine law? Is it placing oneself in a position of total alienation and separateness from the author of our lives? Is it an injurious infringement on the life and well-being of another person or group of persons? Is there wisdom in the affirmation that states, "If we say that we have no sin, we deceive ourselves, and the truth is not in us. If we confess our sins, He is faithful and just to forgive us our sins." But, then, what do we confess, and how genuine can our confession be?

As materials for this book were being compiled and edited the tragedies of 11 September 2001 befell us. A first appropriate response is prayer.

> Save us gracious God, from the dark forces that threaten the lives of your people, in nations and societies and in the human spirit. Deliver us from cynicism and violence, from jealousy and indifference, from fear and despair. We ask this under the guidance of the Holy Spirit and in the name of Jesus Christ the Lord.
>
> [Prayer following Psalm 129 in the *Book of Alternative Services*, slightly adapted.]

We can also consider — in the aftermath of this event — the theological questions that are asked in each of the sections.

✦ What do the categories of sin and grace have to say about these realities?

✦ What nourishes us spiritually during times of societal crisis?

✦ What moral challenges and choices confront us?

Created with free will, we can choose to turn away from God to satisfy our selfish desires, but when we turn to God, following the example of the man, Jesus Christ, we are most truly human.

We are creatures and therefore not initially responsible for our existence. But each of us has been lovingly created with "a mind to know and a heart to love," and that knowledge and love come together in the free will that is also part of our created being — an intrinsic part.

Why are we created with free will? In order to respond to God's initiatives of grace offered to us from birth to death. We are made to be (in **Karl Rahner**'s phrase) "hearers of the word" — God's word. We are made to be open and responsive to the transcendent. But, as we all know too well, our response is not always positive; in fact, all too often we turn away from God's call. There have been and still are those who, observing the near universality of sin, think that sin is part of our created nature. How else to explain it, both in individuals and in societies? There is another answer.

From earliest times Christianity has linked sin to self-centredness. It is explained by the self-love that leads us to over-indulge ourselves, whether physically (greed, inordinate wealth) or spiritually (pride, envy). But that turning to self is as

much an act of the will as is turning to God; and it is the turning to God, not the turning to self, that makes us more truly human. That being said, we must remember that we are made in "the image of God" [Genesis 1:27] and that, as St. Augustine and other saints have known, we can seek and find God within ourselves. But it is *God within self* that we are seeking and finding, the divine self-centre, not merely *self for the sake of self*.

I have said that sin is nearly universal. This is true in the sense that no human person, except Christ, is completely sinless. The "nearly" is to remind us of the countless times human persons have turned away from sin and to God. We often say that we should model ourselves on Christ, but Christ too was tempted, he too chose his path. It was the *man*, Jesus Christ (I am not denying his divinity) who transcended himself to help others. It was the *man*, Jesus Christ, who was open to the will of God, even though it took him to the cross. And we have only to think of the myriads of Christians who, following him, have turned away from their own needs and pleasures to meet the needs of others. They were,

---

KARL RAHNER (1904–1984) was probably the most influential Roman Catholic theologian of the twentieth century. A German Jesuit, he was trained in *The Spiritual Exercises* of Ignatius Loyola and the theology of Thomas Aquinas. Rahner's theology, which became known as "transcendental Thomism," has been called "an ingenious fusion of scholasticism with German idealism and existentialism" [Di Noia, 119]. Like Macquarrie, Rahner based his theology, to a great degree, on experience. He sought to give meaning to Christian doctrines by revealing "how the structures of human existence, as transformed by grace, are the necessary conditions for the experience of Christian faith and life,"

by showing, for example, that the grounds for belief in God are found in human experience of God [Di Noia, 122–123]. Theology had traditionally taught a break or discontinuity between the "natural" and the "supernatural," but Rahner stressed instead the positive relation of the two, insisting that the natural order, specifically the human person, is *open* to God and to grace. Rahner is credited with initiating what has become an axiom of modern theology: "The immanent Trinity is the economic Trinity." His trinitarian theology and his teaching of the universality of grace have provoked debate. Holding several academic posts, Rahner was very much a theologian of the church.

SIN AND GRACE Joanne McWilliam **13**

and are, more, not less, human because they follow Christ's example.

Which way we turn is our own responsibility. Yes, the "goods" offered by sin are attractive, but the good offered by God is infinitely more so.

Our human and Christian minds know this, and our Christian and human know where to offer their love, for, after all, "We love because [God] first loved us" [1 John 4:19].

I fled Him, down the nights and down the days;
I fled Him, down the arches of the years;
I fled Him, down the labyrinthine ways
    Of my own mind; and in the midst of tears
I hid from Him, and under running laughter.
    Up vistaed hopes I sped;
    And shot, precipitated,
Adown Titanic glooms of chasmèd fears,
From those strong Feet that followed, followed after.

From *The Hound of Heaven* by Francis Thompson, 1859–1907.

> **Although we use the word "grace" in many contexts, it always refers to God's gifts to us — gifts of God's free giving, never earned as rewards.**
>
> ROBERT CROUSE

In the broadest sense, the word "grace" (*gratia*) refers to all of God's gifts, freely given (*gratis*) in creation and redemption, the source of all that is beautiful (i.e., "graceful") in nature and in human lives. But the term is used especially to refer to God's free gift of redemption in Jesus Christ, overcoming our alienation, making us *personae gratae* (pleasing) to God. Thus, we speak of "justifying grace": God's free gift of his acceptance of us, for Christ's sake, when we were yet sinners. And we speak of "sanctifying grace," referring to those free gifts of word and sacrament and spiritual community ("means of grace") whereby our lives are continually renewed and transformed.

Christian theology insists that all goodness has its source in God, so that none of us can boast of our merits. As Augustine of Hippo put it, "when God crowns our merits, he crowns nothing but his own gifts." That divine initiative is emphasized in the theory and practice of Christian sacraments — for instance, when an infant is brought to baptism to "receive the fullness of thy grace," or when confirmands come to receive "thy manifold gifts of grace." Sacraments are signs and pledges of grace.

All is God's gift, all is divine initiative; but that does not exclude human responsibility. Hence the church's insistence on faith and penitence as necessary to salutary participation in the sacraments. Yet even faith and penitence must be ascribed to the inspiration of God's grace ("prevenient grace," literally "grace that comes before"), and not to our own virtues. Grace is not a reward for good works. Good works, rather, even the "good work" of faith, are the fruits of grace. "Therefore, we pray that [God's grace] may always prevent [precede us] and follow us, and make us continually to be given to all good works; through Jesus Christ our Lord" [Collect for Trinity XVII, *BCP*].

REFLECTION

Robert quotes the *BCP*'s distinctions between the "fullness of thy grace" given at baptism, and "thy manifold gifts of grace" given in confirmation. How do you see the relationship between the fullness of grace into which we are drawn through baptism into the life, death, and resurrection of Christ, and the particular gifts given through the other sacraments?

Grace, thou source of each perfection,
Favour from the height thy ray;
Thou the star of all direction,
Child of endless truth and day.
From *Hymn 3, Epiphany*
by Christopher Smart, 1722–1771.

Conversion is like falling in love. It reveals sin as an impediment to growth in God's love and at the same time breaks down barriers, so that love floods into us and issues forth in further loving action.

EILEEN SCULLY

Religious conversion is a falling in love. It can happen slowly over time, or in a sudden inbreaking of God's love. It can be a powerful encounter, or it can be, as **John Wesley** described it, a sensation of "my heart being strangely warmed." Conversion opens a journey of discipleship, yet it contains all the moments of discipleship. It is dynamic both because God's love is a living, powerful, transformative force and because we, God's creatures, are living beings, capable of growth, learning, and transformation.

Bernard Lonergan describes the human person as basically open to the divine transcendent. We are *learning* beings. The structure of our learning is a movement from *experience*, which raises questions for us that lead to *insights*. When we assess and seek to understand those insights we exercise *judgement*, and these judgements lead to *decision/action*. Actions turn the wheel to new experiences, which lead to their own insights, judgements, and actions. Each of these points on the wheel corresponds to a part of our consciousness: experience to our emotions, insight to our intelligence, judgement to our capacity to evaluate, decision/action to our capacity to act and make choices in how we live out our commitments, relationships, and power to effect change in the world.

Lonergan argues that conversion is a basic human experience, that healthy human development is open to change/conversion. Such a conversion (like other learning experiences) is felt through our emotions, intelligence, judgement, and actions. This openness requires that we be attentive to our own experiences and that we be attentive to the experiences and stories of others. It requires intelligence to question our experiences. What do they mean? It requires that we weigh our own insights, asking, Are they true? What is their relative importance? How do they stand up compared to the insights of others? And, it requires responsibility for our relationships and actions.

JOHN WESLEY (1703–1791) was an Anglican priest, missionary in the American colonies, and a renowned preacher. He founded the movement called "Methodist," which appealed to the many unchurched by means of rousing sermons and hymns. His approach also emphasized a detailed daily and weekly routine or "method" of study, prayer, and giving, from which his followers came to be known as "Methodists." Condemned by the Church of England authorities, it eventually developed as a separate church. He has been called one of the greatest Christians of his age.

BERNARD LONERGAN (1904–1984), a Canadian Jesuit who taught in Rome, Toronto, and other North American institutions, was and still is very influential in Roman Catholic theology. His overall worldview is set forth in *Grace and Freedom* [1981] and he wrote treatises on the Trinity and Christology as well. His most important contribution, however, was to the theory of knowledge, set forth in *Insight* [1957]. There he presents four "levels" of knowing — gathering data, understanding, judgement, and action and value. *Method* [1972] investigates the different movements of the human spirit and there love is placed above knowledge. A critical edition of Lonergan's works is ongoing [eds. F.E. Crowe and R. Doran] and the journal, *Method*, is devoted to articles on his thought.

Although in religious conversion one may be overwhelmed by the love of God, the illness of original sin is still with us. It may be experienced as an impediment to growth that needs to be confronted, challenged, and transformed. God's love provides the sustaining grace that draws us towards the Creator, in the Spirit and through Christ, and so towards each other and the fullness of being who we were made to be.

A PERSONAL CONVERSION STORY

A teacher once explained the two major understandings of grace to me in this way. There's the medicinal view and the juridical view. In the medicinal (Catholic) understanding, human beings are created good, but the flaw of sin is like a life-threatening illness. We can't get better on our own. Grace appears in the form of the Healer and the medicine the Healer brings. Though the illness will always be there, health returns thanks not only to the medicine, but also to the prescription that tells us how much to take, and to the exercises that give us growing strength to get up, move around, cope with everyday tasks, and finally really enjoy and maintain health. We can't do this on our own: we need others. In turn we will be able to help others and to proclaim this good news. The process is a life of conversion: it is turning to God in every moment for forgiveness and healing and with expressions of gratitude.

Then there's the juridical view. In this more Protestant understanding, humans stand convicted of sin. We are justifiably condemned. But Jesus steps in, takes our place, and tells us to live as the new creation that he has set us free to be and to proclaim this good news. Being convicted and set free occurs all in one moment: this is the conversion that begins a new life.

I've always preferred the medicinal model. But something happened within me when I attended an Indigenous Sacred Circle gathering that left me thinking anew about the possibilities of real life-changing moments.

At the gathering I was witness to the pain, healing, and resurrection of a community of people who were holding each other in healing and hope. The days of the gathering were to me like drips of warm water on an iceberg. I was very conscious of being confronted by God's presence and of understanding God's nearness more than ever before. I can only describe the experience as new. The healing service was intensely frightening and awesome. In it I was confronted by what racism and hatred were in my heart. I was also confronted by my urge to control and oppress, with the ways in which I've used power over people, and with the defensive barriers that I put up to block the love of God.

As I sat for healing prayers and was asked, "What do you ask of our Creator?", I named a heart that was hardened and frozen and in need of healing. During prayers the sensation was of powerful, physical, warming love. It was as though all the stopped-up valves were opened and the warmth in my heart could flow freely for the first time since I was a very young child.

At last the healing within myself could begin. I would name this a significant conversion.

REFLECTION

David Religious experience abounds these days, but we rarely talk about "conversion." Perhaps it smacks too much of revival meetings. Your paper reminds me of the complex nature of the phenomenon: it is *psychological*, it is *religious*, it is *Christian*.

Revivalism tends to define conversion in terms of being "born again." Its historical development suggests that it was an over-reaction to the masses of nominal baptized Christians who showed little sign of authentic faith.

In a non-revivalist world, it is easy to dismiss the role of conversion in people's lives. It is most often gradual, but that does not mean that gradual conversion is better than conversions resulting from crisis. I think that in the future we will encounter more new Christians who arrive at our churches with stories of crisis experience.

A responsible pastoral response will be to not dismiss these persons as victims of over-stimulated emotions, but to help these converts weave their stories into the gospel story, to see the experience as the work of the Holy Spirit, leading them to Jesus.

✦ Conversion seems to have many faces, moments, and movements. How would you describe your own experience(s) (if any) of conversion?

NOURISHED BY GRACE

The Sacraments

KEY POINTS

- ✦ Grace is the antidote to sin. It is the gift of God.
- ✦ The sacraments, prayer, contemplation, and action may all be considered as both means of grace and results of grace.
- ✦ Each individual Christian needs to find a balance between private and corporate prayer, and among contemplation, prayer, sacraments, and action.
- ✦ Pilgrimage is a traditional metaphor for the Christian life.

Anglican formularies are clear that the sacraments are given to us by God as effectual means of grace, and that our cooperation is necessary for the grace to work. The church continues to pose questions about the sacraments.

ROBERT CROUSE

"Sacraments ordained by Christ be not only badges or token of Christian men's profession, but rather they be certain sure witnesses, and effectual signs of grace, and God's good will towards us, by the which he doth work invisibly in us, and doth not only quicken, but also strengthen and confirm our Faith in him . . . .

"The Sacraments were not ordained of Christ to be gazed upon, or to be carried about, but that we should duly use them. And in such only as worthily receive the same they have a wholesome effect or operation: but they that receive them unworthily purchase to themselves damnation, as Saint Paul saith" [Articles of Religion XXV].

According to the Catechism in the *Book of Common Prayer*, a sacrament is "an outward and visible sign of an inward and spiritual grace, given to us by Christ himself, as a means whereby we receive this grace, and a pledge to assure us thereof" [*BCP*, 550]. Conforming to this definition, there are two sacraments "generally necessary to salvation; that is to say, Baptism, and the Supper of the Lord, which is the Holy Communion" [ibid.]. As the Elizabethan theologian, **Bishop Jewel**, observes, there have been variations in reckoning the number of sacraments; but these, he says, are "difference of opinion that standeth in terms rather than in the matter."

> Do we refuse confirmation, penance, orders, and matrimony? Is there no use of these among us? Do we not allow them? Yes, for we do confirm, and teach repentance, and minister holy orders, and account matrimony and so use it, as an honourable state of life. We visit the sick among us, and anoint them with the precious oil of the mercy of God. But we call not these sacraments, because they have not the like institution [*Treatise on the Sacraments, Works* II, 1102–03].

In any case, whether we employ a broader or a narrower definition of "sacrament," as **Richard Hooker** (please see explanatory note on page 42) remarks, "We find grace expressly mentioned as their true essential form, elements as the matter whereunto that form doth enjoin itself" [*Laws* V.58.3]. Thus, they are outward signs of that "saving grace which Christ originally is or hath for the general good of his whole Church," which "by sacraments he severally deriveth unto every member thereof" [V.57.5].

JOHN JEWEL (1522–1571) was an intellectual leader in the English Reformation, noted particularly for his *An Apology of the Church of England*, a defence of the Anglican settlement against both Roman Catholic and Puritan criticisms. From 1560 he was Bishop of Salisbury. Richard Hooker was among his pupils.

Thus, sacraments are instruments of God's grace, whereby the benefits of Christ's atoning sacrifice are extended to each participant; whereby his death becomes the source of our new birth (baptism), strengthens us for Christian life and witness (confirmation), and nourishes us for eternal life in his kingdom (eucharist); whereby our lives are ordered to his service (ordination and matrimony), and we receive forgiveness (penance) and healing (unction). The sacraments constitute a system corresponding to, and sanctifying all the stages and conditions of our humanity. At the centre of that system is the eucharist, because in that sacrament there is made present to us that saving work of Christ on Calvary, whence all those varied graces flow.

EDWARD REYNOLDS (1599–1676) in his early life was sympathetic to the Puritan movement, but later conformed to the Church of England and worked to bring about a reconciliation between it and the Puritans. From 1661 Reynolds was Bishop of Norwich. He was also the author of many devotional works that had a lasting popularity.

As Bishop Jewel puts it, "We feed not the people of God with bare Signs and Figures, but teach them that the sacraments of Christ be Holy Mysteries, and that in the ministration thereof Christ is set before us, even as He was crucified upon the Cross" [*Reply to Harding, Works* I, 448]. And, as Richard Hooker explains,

> We take not baptism nor the eucharist as bare resemblances or memorials of things absent, neither for naked signs and testimonies of grace received before, but (as they are indeed and in verity) for means effectual whereby God, when we take the sacraments, delivereth into our hands that grace available unto eternal life which grace the sacraments represent or signify [*Laws* V.57.5].

Sacraments are, in the first place, God's gifts, not inventions of the Christian community. But they are not magical devices, and their effects depend upon the intentions and dispositions of the participants [see 1 Corinthians 11:27–29]. The validity of sacraments depends upon the *appropriate minister* (for example, bishops in ordination, priests in eucharist), *validly ordained*, and *intending to minister* Christ's sacraments. But, as the Thirty-Nine Articles indicate, the validity of sacraments does *not* depend upon *the personal worthiness* of the minister. They are "effectual, because of Christ's institution and promise, although they be ministered by evil men" [see Article XXVI].

We may conclude with the words of the Caroline divine, **Bishop Edward Reynolds** (1599–1676):

> So then, in general, the nature of a Sacrament is to be representative of a Substance, the sign of a covenant, the seal of a purchase, the figure of a body, the witness of our faith, the earnest of our hope, the presence of things distant, the sight of things absent, the taste of things inconceivable, and the knowledge of things that are past knowledge [*Meditations on the Holy Sacrament. Works* III, 19].

REFLECTION

David When sacraments, ministered or received, are thought to be magical, we must be reminded that the spiritual benefits of sacraments are not automatic. God is present when the sacrament is received in faith, but is free to be present in judgement when that faith is absent, or when the reception of the sacrament is turned to ulterior motives [see 1 Corinthians 11:27–29].

BAPTISM IN THE NEW TESTAMENT

Edith Humphrey

Jesus, in his baptism, plunged into the centre of our fallen world, identifying freely with its suffering and death, and showing himself to be the uniquely "beloved one" of God, one who "takes away the sin of the world" and "baptizes in the Spirit" [John 1:29–34]. In his baptism he identified with us; in ours we identify with him; we "are buried with him ... in order that we too may live a new life" [Romans 6:3–4]. To be baptized means, then, to be united with this One "with whom [God] is pleased" [Mark 1:11].

Both the gospels and Paul speak of baptism as an effective event, as accomplishing God's own purpose [see Matthew 3:15; Romans 6:4–5]. Yet the Scriptures also point out that the life that follows is not automatically Christ-like, but must be cultivated. Immediately after his baptism Jesus is driven by the Spirit into the wilderness, there to re-enact Adam's time of trial, this time successfully. So too the baptized Christian is to count herself or himself "dead to sin, but alive to God in Christ Jesus" [Romans 6:11]. This new life involves ongoing decisions to thwart sin's usurping desire to rule again and, instead, to offer oneself in thankfulness to God [see Romans 6:12–14]. This new life is never lived alone, but through the Spirit who joins in our baptism and in the strengthening company of the baptized [see Ephesians 4:4–13].

Churches today differ on when baptism should be administered. The Scriptures are silent on the question of infant baptism, except to note that in early days whole households were baptized. Some see infant baptism as the sign of God's active initiative in our midst, and adult baptism as the sign that speaks of human response. Anglican tradition observes both forms, remembering that in Jesus' own baptism, as in his complete life, death, and resurrection, divine initiative and human response meet in perfect harmony.

GRACE IN BAPTISM

Eileen Scully

"Christian baptism is rooted in the ministry of Jesus of Nazareth, in his death and resurrection. It is incorporation into Christ, who is the crucified and risen Lord; it is entry into the New Covenant between God and God's people. Baptism is a gift of God, and is administered in the name of the Father, the Son and the Holy Spirit" [*Baptism, Eucharist and Ministry:* Faith & Order Paper No. 111, World Council of Churches, 1982].

My extended family includes a number of different Christian traditions, the dominant being Anglican and Mennonite-Anabaptist. Animated discussions about infant baptism and believer's baptism crop up from time to time. When it gets down to the theological nuts and bolts of it, though, there is surprising agreement, as well as acknowledgement that each tradition has tended to emphasize different aspects of the truth. While Anglicans in the family have emphasized the *receiving* of grace in baptism, Anabaptists have emphasized the *taking on* of the responsibilities of faith. In truth, these are two parts of the same sacramental reality.

Baptism is first and foremost the gift of the call of God's grace: God's initiative drawing us away from the alienation and destruction of sin into the life, death, and resurrection of Jesus Christ. There is in baptism, whether of an infant, child, or adult, a heightened sense of dependence on God's grace and on the community. When we are given a name in baptism, it is a sign of *who* we are and *whose* we are. Our belonging is twofold: I am God's child, so named; I am also baptized into the body in which all members belong each to the other.

Baptism is also about response — not just my own (though it certainly is that) nor that of my parents and sponsors (though it is also that), but of this whole body, the church. In Christ we are made a new creation and brought into new life — a life shaped by baptismal rhythms. Over and over again in our lives, God calls us and confronts us in love. Over and over again we are shown our sin, and we repent and are forgiven. Over and over again we are pulled into walking with Jesus through the patterns of his life, his ministry, his risk-taking, his loving self-giving, grieving, and healing. Over and over again we experience many small deaths and resurrections, until ultimately, like Jesus, we face our own future in God's hands. Over and over again we celebrate the faith, hope, and love that are gift and nourishment to us.

These are the rhythms of the baptismal life. We do not walk them alone, but together in this body we call church. The waters of baptism unite us not just around one font in one building; they draw us into a river of waters that have been flowing for two millienia, binding us in a community that extends both through time and through space.

The Baptismal Covenant
Book of Alternative Services

✦ Will you continue in the apostles' teaching and fellowship, in the breaking of bread, and in the prayers?

✦ Will you persevere in resisting evil and, whenever you fall into sin, repent and return to the Lord?

✦ Will you proclaim by word and example the good news of God in Christ?

✦ Will you seek and serve Christ in all persons, loving your neighbour as yourself?

✦ Will you strive for justice and peace among all people, and respect the dignity of every human being?

THE EUCHARIST

New Testament and Early Church

The eucharist, the church's fundamental and central act of thanksgiving, has been a part of Christian life since New Testament times. It is generally agreed that, after the resurrection, the disciples continued the tradition of eating together, following the pattern of Jewish fellowship meals. The primitive church, however, saw more in this than a community gathered in peace.

In various accounts of the Last Supper we find different themes that were later woven together. Mark and Matthew give it strong overtones suggesting the end of all time: Jesus says, "Never again shall I drink from the fruit of the vine until that day when I drink it new in the kingdom of God" [Mark 14:25]. Their accounts link the Last Supper closely with Christ's death in the words of institution: "For this is my blood, the blood of the covenant, shed for many for the forgiveness of sins" [Matthew 26:28]. Luke and Paul bring the idea of commemoration, and in Paul we find Christ's command to continue the meals together after his death: "Do this in memory of me" [1 Corinthians 11:24f]. It has been suggested that here Paul was conveying his understanding that this fellowship meal was the mode of Christ's continuing presence in the community [Price and Weil, 187].

Although Christ's death was early understood as a **sacrifice,** this term was not applied to the eucharist in the New Testament. However, there are hints of sacrifice in the institution narratives of the synoptic gospels, and in certain Pauline texts: for example, "We have been justified by Christ's blood" [Romans 5:9]. Although the inference of sacrifice is there, it was only in the third century that the sacrifice of the cross is explicitly associated, by Cyprian of Carthage, with the eucharistic sacrifice of thanksgiving. Augustine gave an ecclesial dimension to the sacrifice — the people of God offer themselves individually and corporally with, in, and through Christ. This dimension of the eucharist is reflected in the *Book of Common Prayer* when we say:

SACRIFICE The word 'sacrifice' has religious roots. It means 'to make [something] holy' by offering it to God, by placing it therefore in the realm of the holy. It is this offering of something to God which is the essence of the sacrifice, but, because the offering (in pagan and Hebrew sacrifices) so often involved slaughter, the idea of propitiation of an angry Deity became associated with sacrifice. Spinning off from that, we tend to think of sacrifice negatively, suffering, a giving-up of something for whatever reason.

But John Macquarrie and others argue that Christian theology has been too negative in its explanations of Christ's sacrifice by its constant use of the language of satisfaction, expiation, and ransom. Hugh Blenkin (cited Macquarrie, 136) states that true sacrifice is life-giving (we remember that the blood smeared on the doorposts in the first Passover was a signal to spare that family). Our Christian focus should be on Christ's death as the source of the new life which it brings.

In the eucharistic sacrifice we offer to God an offering which is already holy. We do not, cannot, repeat the sacrifice, and we certainly cannot add to it. The sacrifice of Christ is re-presented "in such a way that a past event is recalled and experienced so that its significance and power are known and felt as if the event were present" (Macquarrie, 140).

And here we offer and present unto thee, O Lord, ourselves, our souls and bodies, to be a reasonable, holy, and living sacrifice unto thee [85].

It appears also in the *Book of Alternative Services:*

Unite us to your Son in his sacrifice, that we, made acceptable in him, may be sanctified by the Holy Spirit [Eucharistic Prayer 3].

And again:

Gracious God, with this bread and wine we celebrate the death and resurrection of Jesus, and we offer ourselves to you in him [Eucharistic Prayer 5].

The Medieval Church

The early church, like the ancient world generally, understood a symbol to partake of the reality it symbolized, but over the centuries symbols came to be seen as no more than signs. An example may help to clarify the difference. An arrow pointing left gives information; if it is defaced or obscured, we may be annoyed, but feel no sense of outrage. It is a sign. But to burn or trample upon the flag of a country is rightly seen as an insult to the country itself. The flag partakes of the reality it symbolizes. Over the same period, the "Body of Christ" shifted in meaning from the church to the consecrated elements of bread and wine.

The eucharist is no longer perceived as a community celebration but as a ritual drama enacted by the priest at the altar, and the congregation become merely spectators. Similarly, the bread and wine of the eucharist are no longer seen as the symbols of participation in the risen Christ through the sharing of a meal, but as sacred objects on the altar [Crockett, 107].

Attention thus came to focus on how the eucharistic elements could be at the same time bread and wine and the body and blood of Christ. Some insisted that the bread and wine are identical with Christ's *historical* (rather than his *risen*) body. Thomas Aquinas himself did not hold this physically realist theory; for him the sacramental body was spiritual or mystic. He shared the patristic understanding of symbol/sacrament, and he worked out a theory in which the substance of the bread and wine were changed but their appearance remained the same. For him that substance was both *real* and *spiritual*; only the bread and wine were physical. His doctrine, however, "was widely misunderstood in a physical or materialistic sense" [Crockett, 119]. It came to be the official eucharistic theology of the Roman Catholic Church and to be understood synonymously with "real presence."

The Anglican Reformation

The Anglican Church has traditionally held that Christ is truly present in the eucharist, and that the presence is spiritual, not material. Given these two premises there has been room for considerable variety in eucharistic theology. Richard Hooker states:

> Let it therefore be sufficient for me presenting myself at the Lord's table to know what there I receive from him, without searching or inquiring how Christ performeth his promise. ...What these elements are in themselves it skilleth not [makes no difference], it is enough that to me who take them they are the body and blood of Christ [*Laws* V.76.12, quoted Crockett, 178].

Crockett goes on to say that this agnosticism concerning the *manner* of Christ's presence in the eucharist and "receptionism" prevailed in Anglicanism until the Tractarian Movement. He continues:

> It is important to remember, however, that "receptionism" is a doctrine of the real presence, but a doctrine that relates the real presence primarily to the worthy receiver rather than to the elements of bread and wine [190].

"Worthy receiver" might seem to imply that it is the faith of the communicant that effects the change, but the flow is entirely the other way. That the elements become the body and blood of Christ is the work of divine grace, not human faith.

The intent of **Thomas Cranmer** and of Hooker in the sixteenth century and of other seventeenth-century theologians was to shift the emphasis of the eucharist away from the remote adoration prevalent in the Middle Ages and back to spiritual nourishment. Gradually over the seventeenth century a heightened sacramental spirituality grew and the theme of sacrifice reappeared. The eucharist was and still is seen to be a memorial sacrifice of thanksgiving that adds nothing to the sacrifice of the cross. This understanding is reflected in the words of the *Book of Common Prayer*:

> ... who made there, by his one oblation of himself *once offered* a full, perfect, and sufficient sacrifice, oblation, and satisfaction, for the sins of the whole world... [Prayer of Consecration, italics added].

and in the *Book of Alternative Services:*

> Gracious God, his *perfect* sacrifice destroys the power of sin and death [Eucharistic Prayer 1, italics added].

Both the Wesleyan and the Tractarian movements contributed to the development of eucharistic theology. The former allied the sac-

THOMAS CRANMER (1489–1556) was a scholar, diplomat, civil servant, Archbishop of Canterbury, and finally a martyr. He believed in the supremacy of the state over the church and was appointed to Canterbury to facilitate Henry VIII's divorce from Catherine of Aragon. He was burned in the reign of Queen Mary for denying the *physical* presence of Christ in the eucharist. Cranmer is best remembered as the chief architect of the *Book of Common Prayer* (1549, 1552). It reflects his theology and its language is a precious heritage of the Anglican Church.

rament to evangelism as a means of grace. The latter emphasized the sacramental principle that, in a manner analogous to the incarnation, divine grace is given through natural, material means. Where the Tractarians differed from most of their predecessors was in their insistence that the presence of Christ was brought about by the words of consecration and is thereafter objectively present in the elements, apart from communion. While the Tractarians taught this objective presence, they also taught that Christ "is present *in grace* only to those who receive him in faith." [Crockett, 217, italics added] Both the Wesleyans and the Tractarians tied their eucharistic theology closely to issues of social justice:

> Here, Lord, we take the broken bread
> and drink the wine, believing
> that by thy life our souls are fed,
> thy parting gifts receiving.
>
> As thou hast given, so we would give
> ourselves for others' healing;
> as thou has lived, so we would live,
> the Father's love revealing.
>
> *Charles Venn Pilcher* (1879–1961)

The eucharistic doctrine in the Prayer Book has been the wellspring of Anglican eucharistic thought and practice.

THE EUCHARIST IN THE BOOK OF COMMON PRAYER

Robert Crouse

The service of Holy Communion or Holy Eucharist as it appears in the 1962 Canadian revision of the *Book of Common Prayer* descends, through several revisions, from "the Supper of the Lorde and the Holy Communion Commonly Called the Masse" in the first English Prayer Book of 1549. Archbishop Cranmer, chief architect of that book and of its revision in 1552, together with his colleagues, had the delicate task of balancing the claims of ancient Catholic tradition with the ideals of the Reformation, to ensure the service's conformity to the clear word of God in Holy Scripture, and to encourage devout participation, edification, and more frequent communion.

The doctrinal principles informing the reformed liturgy are most clearly expressed in Archbishop Cranmer's own writings on the subject, especially in his treatise *On the True and Catholic Doctrine of the Lord's Supper*. Against a superstitiously materialistic notion of Christ's presence in the sacrament, Cranmer insists on both the reality of the presence and the spiritual character of it:

> The same flesh that was given in Christ's last supper was given also upon the cross and is given daily in the ministration of the sacrament [24].
>
> I do not say that Christ's body and blood be given to us in signification and not in deed. But I do as plainly speak as I can, that

Christ's body and blood be given to us in deed, yet not corporally and carnally, but spiritually and effectually [37].

And again:

Through grace there is a spiritual mutation by the mighty power of God, so that he who worthily eateth of that bread, doth spiritually eat Christ, and dwelleth in Christ and Christ in him [276].

The corporate dimension of the communion is emphasized, for in this sacrament is represented and fulfilled the unity of the church.

As the bread and wine which we do eat be turned into our flesh and blood; even so be all faithful Christians turned into the body of Christ, and so be joined to Christ, and also together among themselves, that they do make one mystical body of Christ, as St Paul saith: "We have one bread and one body, as many as be partakers of one bread and one cup" [42].

The focal point of the liturgy is the commemoration of the atoning sacrifice of Christ on Calvary, whence all these blessings flow. The eucharist is indeed a sacrifice, and yet it adds nothing to Christ's "one oblation of himself once offered."

There is but one such sacrifice, whereby our sins be pardoned, and God's mercy and favour obtained, which is the death of the Son of God, our Lord Jesu Christ [346].

The eucharist is the effectual memorial of that one sacrifice. Nor is it the offering of the priest alone: when the priest makes the memorial of that one oblation,

He doth it in the name of the people; so that sacrifice is no more the priest's than the people's....The priest should declare the death and passion of Christ, and all the people should look upon the cross in the Mount of Calvary.... And this is the priest's and people's sacrifice, not to be propitiators for sin, but ... to worship continually in mystery that which was once offered for the price of sin [359].

Cranmer continues:

Wherefore "every man," as St Paul saith, "must examine himself" when he shall approach to that holy table ... wherein we be taught that we spiritually feed upon Christ ... although he be in heaven at his Father's right hand....We should understand the sacrament not carnally, but spiritually.... Being like eagles in this life, we should fly up to heaven in our hearts, where that Lamb is resident ... by whose passion we are filled at his table [378, 398].

And now, O Father, mindful of the love
that bought us, once for all on Calvary's tree,
and having with us him that pleads above,
we here present, we here spread forth to thee
that only offering perfect in thine eyes,
that one, true, pure immortal sacrifice.

Look, Father, on his anointed face,
and only look on us as found in him;
look not on our misgivings of thy grace,
our prayers so languid and our prayers so dim.
For lo! Between our sins and their reward
we set the passion of thy Son, our Lord.

Canon William Bright (1824–1901)

THE EUCHARIST IN THE BOOK OF ALTERNATIVE SERVICES

Walter Deller

Because of the tension and controversy surrounding the introduction of the *Book of Alternative Services,* it will likely be very difficult to achieve any objective assessment of its theology and impact for at least another forty years. These notes will be, in part, an exercise in experiential theology, based on an experience of worshipping with the *BAS* contemporary rite.

What might be noted, first off, is that the overt theology of the *BAS* is that *the normative weekly service of the Anglican community is the eucharist.* The eucharist forms the backbone for the baptismal rite, and most other rites included in the book. This centrality of the eucharist is the result of a process going back at least as far as the Oxford movement in the nineteenth century, and developed throughout the twentieth century by such groups as the **Associated Parishes** and the introduction of family communion. For many Anglican parishes this was theological news in a practical sense — the centrality of the eucharist in the *Book of Alternative Services* disrupted and displaced long traditions of mattins as the main service on Sunday.

In more specific ways, one might argue that the *BAS* eucharist draws more attention than the *BCP* to *the centrality of Easter* for Christian life. This connects with a greater emphasis on connecting the present community with its eschatological future and reality in the risen life of Christ, present particularly in the eucharistic prayers of the *BAS*.

I think it would be correct to argue that the shape and rituals of the *BAS* eucharist place a greater emphasis on *the gathered community of the faithful*. One notes this in the explicit naming of the opening part of the services as "The Gathering of the Community," in the principle of drawing readers from the congregation, in the general hand-shaking and greeting that accompanies the peace, in the ritual practice of having the gifts of bread and wine brought to the altar by members of the community from somewhere in the assembly at the offertory, and by the introduction of more responsive elements in the structure of the eucharistic prayers. An interesting example in this regard has been the *BAS*'s unpopular excision of the Prayer of Humble Access (in the *BCP* almost the only element in the prayers around the communion portion of the liturgy said by all the people). But the introduction of the doxology from Ephesians as one of the options for prayers after communion has

proven the single most powerful and striking success of the *BAS* ritual, reawakening people to the power of this passage from scripture. This doxology has moved rapidly into the realm of the "common prayer" of gathered Anglicans as a way to end meetings and events.

The other place where, in practice, the *BAS* eucharistic rite manifests a rich theology of the gathered community is at the "Prayers of the People," where the loosely structured forms suggested by the rubrics and even the various forms of litany provided elsewhere in the book create *more space for the inclusion of the hopes, concerns and prayers of the entire community.*

The shifting of the Peace to precede the offertory in the *BAS* ritual, and the general movement that goes with it, has had the effect on congregations of *creating more movement among the faithful toward one another.* It also offers a mechanism for greeting strangers. This behaviour gives rise to a more explicit theology: many Anglicans now behave as if we believe that we ought to be a welcoming and embracing community in which we express physically and verbally our sense of

---

ASSOCIATED PARISHES was founded in 1946 "by a group of [American] clergy who were in despair over eleven o'clock Sunday morning." They and other priests began to use their parishes as laboratories for the liturgical movement in the Episcopal Church. Their first goal was to restore the eucharist as the main service on Sunday in which people participated actively. The daily office was to be celebrated every day in church; and baptisms, marriages, and funerals were to be public events. Fellowship around the altar extended to parish life. In addition to the vestry, an AP parish was to have a parish council with committees for evangelism,

education, worship, stewardship, and house and grounds. AP also sought to forge links between the liturgy and social issues such as racial justice and the use of property. In the 1960s the Associated Parishes began to urge the need for a new Book of Common Prayer, and supported trial use of new and revised liturgies. In recent years its activities have broadened to renewal of the diaconate and the catechumenate, and advocacy for the use of inclusive language. [Adapted from the Associated Parishes website at www.associatedparishes.org.]

being in touch with one another and caring about one another.

I will not comment extensively on the eucharistic prayers, as much ink has been spilled over them already. One particularly controversial question has been the use of an **epiclesis** in the newer prayers. This would be one example of several linkages with Roman Catholic and Orthodox liturgies. One resulting theological impact of the *BAS,* for Anglicans who use it, has been to make them more aware of *our church as an ecumenical church.*

There is *much more emphasis on sin* in the *BAS* eucharistic prayers than in the *BCP.* The *BCP* eucharistic prayer presents sin in its broad all-inclusive aspect: "sins of the whole world"; "for you and for many for the remission of sins"; "we and all they whole Church may obtain remission of our sins" and as expunged primarily through Christ's death on the Cross. The *BAS* eucharistic prayers present a much more dramatic view of sin as a reality and force in which we are all caught up, through which we have made wrong choices and to which the entire life, death, and resurrection of Jesus Christ is God's response. The six eucharistic prayers offer a rich range of language.

+ "When we turned away from you in sin;"
+ "His perfect sacrifice destroys the power of sin and death;
+ "That he might shatter the chains of evil and death and banish the darkness of sin and despair";
+ "In him, you have brought us out of error into truth, out of sin into righteousness, out of death into life";
+ "But we turn against you and betray your trust; and we turn against one another";
+ "But we rebel against you by the evil we do";
+ "Betrayed and forsaken, he did not strike back.... On the cross he defeated the power of sin and death";
+ "When our disobedience took us far from you, you did not abandon us to the power of death."

That said, my cumulative experience has been that the *BAS* eucharist is *an act of rejoicing and glorification of God for the work of Jesus Christ in the redemption of the whole world and the gift of the Holy Spirit which empowers us to live faithfully in Christ.* I often find myself in tears at the conclusion of Eucharist Prayer 3:

> In the fullness of time, reconcile all things in Christ, and make them new, and bring us to that city of light where you dwell with all your sons and daughters; through Jesus

THE EPICLESIS is the part of the prayer of consecration that invokes the Holy Spirit. In the *Book of Common Prayer* it is "And we pray that by the power of the Holy Spirit, all we who are partakers of this holy Communion may be fulfilled with thy grace and heavenly benediction." The *Book of Alternative Services* has a different one for each eucharistic prayer. "Send your Holy Spirit upon us and upon these gifts, that all who eat and drink at this table may be one body and one holy people, a living sacrifice in Jesus Christ, our Lord" (#1). "We pray you, gracious God, to send your Holy Spirit upon these gifts, that they may be the sacrament of the body of Christ and his blood of the new covenant" (#3). "Send your Holy Spirit on us and on these gifts, that we may know the presence of Jesus in the breaking of the bread, and share in the life of the family of your children" (#5).

Christ our Lord, the firstborn of all creation, the head of the Church and the author of our salvation; by whom, and with whom, and in whom, in the unity of the Holy Spirit, all honour and glory are yours, almighty father, now and for ever.

These words resonate with the Bible I read every day, with the cadences of the *BCP* from which I first learned to pray as an Anglican, with other Christian liturgies, music, and art I have come to love over the years, and they teach me to hope for something beyond all present hope or belief.

SOME QUESTIONS ABOUT "SACRIFICE" IN THE LITURGY

David Reed

What do we mean when we ritually process the bread and wine to the table at the offertory? I know that liturgical ceremony does not live by hard and fast rules, as our variegated history shows. Sometimes ritual practices simply overpower the intended meaning of the rite (text). But here we may ask if there is a *shift or change* in the meaning, at least in emphasis.

Various meanings of "offering" and "sacrifice" come together in the liturgy. There is the offering of our "alms and oblations" (offering) when *money* is collected for the church and the poor. This is followed by the prayer of consecration that acknowledges *Christ's* "full, perfect, and sufficient sacrifice, oblation, and satisfaction, for the sins of the whole world." Third, we "do make"

the act of *eucharist* in which we beseech God "to accept this our sacrifice of praise and thanksgiving." Finally, there is the offering of *ourselves*, whereby we "offer and present unto thee, O Lord, ourselves, our souls and bodies, to be a reasonable, holy, and living sacrifice unto thee...."

The ways in which the offering is received and the elements (bread and wine) presented have varied over time. But seldom have they been ritualized with both acts occurring at the same time before communion. The convergence in this moment of the collection, the elements, and the presenters conveys meaning.

It may simply mean that representatives of the church are presenting the fruits of their labour in money and the symbols of the good creation offered to God for transformation. But it also may easily symbolize the offering of *ourselves* to God. If so, is this act not out of order with what we want to say and the Prayer Book has always intended about grace and the eucharist as a gospel sacrament, an act that precedes anything we can do to overcome our human condition? For example, the familiar words of the *Book of Common Prayer* at the offertory, "All things come of thee, O Lord, and of thine own have we given thee," were dropped precisely because they were seen as pre-empting the oblation of Christ.

Certainly, there are no words spoken during the transfer of the elements. But words have been replaced by a ritual act that may speak more loudly, in a way that obscures the real meaning, Christ's full and sufficient sacrifice for us. Our sacrifice can first of all be only a humble and joyous response to the sacrifice of Christ on our behalf. And only then can we offer "our souls and bodies." This appropriately occurs *after* the consecration, not at the offertory.

All this may be irrelevant, except that we live in a culture that still needs to hear that salvation is not the result of its own achievement. With that in mind, clarity about God's saving grace in Christ is not religious narrow-mindedness but an act of love.

PENANCE

Joanne McWilliam Penance marks the church's pastoral recognition of penitence, sincere regret for turning away from God, and a firm resolve to turn again Godwards. It has a long history in the church, beginning as a public (both in admission of sin and the reconciliation of the penitent) ceremony in the early centuries. Hard conditions (penance means "punishment") stretching over a considerable period of time were laid upon the returning Christian. This system fell into disuse (for one reason, it limited penance to once in a lifetime, causing many to delay baptism until fully mature [Augustine of Hippo], or even until the deathbed [Constantine]). Gradually, in the early Middle Ages, "auricular" or private confession to one priest took its place. This practice in turn was abandoned by the churches of the Protestant Reformation, but it has been retained by Anglicans in the Oxford/Tractarian Movement tradition.

Victoria Matthews "All may, none must, some should" is the Anglican description of the practice of auricular confession. To this we often add "few do."

It is thought by many that the inclusion of a general confession and absolution in (almost) every liturgy replaces/helps us to avoid the practice of private confession. Nevertheless, it is thought by those in the Tractarian/High church tradition that accountability is helpful and the actual practice of preparation for confession good discipline. Almost all Anglicans recognize the great helpfulness of confession in times of particular consciousness of sinfulness. In recent years the discipline of the fifth step in the AA has helped make the practice of confession acceptable in broad church circles.

The Anglican view of the penance assigned by the priest is that it is the first great act of thanksgiving for the forgiveness of one's sins by God. (This is quite different from Roman Catholic theology, as I understand it.) Anglicans understand the presence of a priest (or, according to the *BAS*, a deacon or lay person) as drawing attention to the corporate aspect of confession. The confession restores us to the community of which priest and penitent are both members.

In terms of frequency of practice, there is no real standard. For those who seek out confession very occasionally (once or twice in a lifetime), their need is geared by a troubled conscience rather than (as with Roman Catholics) the seriousness of the sin committed. Those who consider it part of their spiritual discipline would seek out their confessor not less frequently than once a year.

CONFIRMATION

Robert Crouse

In traditional Anglican theology and pastoral practice, confirmation has been regarded as an element in a process of initiation, whereby a Christian baptized in infancy takes on personal responsibility for those baptismal promises, receives gifts of the Holy Spirit for life as a mature Christian, and is therefore prepared to receive the Holy Communion in a spirit of faith and penitence. For that reason, Anglicans have regarded Confirmation as the normal (although not absolute) prerequisite for receiving Holy Communion [*BCP*, 561].

Although by no means always consistently administered, that threefold pattern of initiation has been the practice of Western Christendom from late antiquity to the present day (see, for example, *Catechism of the Catholic Church*, 1992, sections 1317–1322, where the traditional practice of infant baptism, confirmation at "the age of reason," and then reception of Holy Communion is insisted upon). The practice of Eastern Christendom has been somewhat different, administering all three initiatory rites at one ceremony, normally to infants, employing chrism blessed by the bishop.

During the last century, the meaning of these initiatory rites was the subject of much controversy, giving rise to substantial variations in Anglican practice, especially in regard to confirmation and first communion (see, for example, our Canadian *BAS*). There are basic questions involved. Is confirmation in any sense a "completion" of baptism? Is the presence of the bishop (or chrism) necessary for confirmation? Is confirmation (like baptism and ordination) once for all, or is it repeatable? To what extent is conscious commitment important for the efficacy of a sacrament? Is confirmation (or, at least, the conscious commitment it involves) prerequisite to communicant status?

REFLECTION

David The recent trend to discourage confirmation as primarily a spiritual stage of commitment for early teens is, it seems to me, a mixed blessing. It has the benefit of prying the church's practice free from the cultural notion that confirmation is simply a rite of passage. But what concerns me is that it is also just one more moment when we yet again say "no" to our youth. Instead of exploring effective ways to deepen the faith of our young people, we have largely ignored them, leaving a massive generational gap in the pews. I wonder if Confirmation has the power any longer to address our situation, and I worry that sound alternatives are not yet on the horizon.

Victoria I suspect the current nervousness, and sometimes even distaste, about the sacrament of confirmation stems from our hesitation to do anything that would minimize baptism. As all ministry is rooted in baptism, there are some who fear suggesting that anything could add to or enhance the gift of baptism.

Secondly, as Robert Crouse has stated, there is an emphasis in rites for confirmation upon personal responsibility. The baptismal covenant of the *BAS* is a fine document, but, as long as the majority of those presented for Christian initiation are infants, it is easy to minimize personal responsibility. Confirmation of those of the age of reason (another fine item for debate) clearly implies that serious discipleship is expected, and that doesn't sit well in a society that is wary of religious commitment.

So where does that leave us? Unlike those who rejoice to quip that confirmation is a rite in search of theology, and those others who say it is a poor rite of passage but the best we have so let's not lose it, I believe confirmation is not only the strengthening of the Holy Spirit through the laying on of hands by prayer, but an opportunity for serious formation for Christian discipleship.

MATRIMONY

David Reed

The Anglican Church of Canada understands matrimony to be the lifelong union between a man and woman marked by mutual vows. Scripture says that they become "one flesh" [Genesis 2:24, Mark 10:7–8] in a deep personal bond that defines the nature of the relationship between them and calls them to grow together spiritually, emotionally, and bodily.

Matrimony is a universal institution, "to be honourable among all [people]" [*BCP*, 564], though certainly not a requirement laid upon all individuals. It is sacred in that it was "instituted by God" [see *BCP*, 564] and is thereby promised God's enabling grace. For this reason the Prayer Book calls matrimony one of the "commonly called Sacraments" [*BCP*, Article XXV, 708]. Paul describes it as a sign of the union between Christ and his church (see Ephesians 5:21–33), which may be interpreted as extending to marriage the marks of the covenantal relationship established by God.

Marital love is intended for both human flourishing and a witnessing to the nature of God's love for the world. Lifelong faithfulness reflects God's unconditional love, provides a stable community in good times and bad, and promises the potential for mutual growth in affection and intimacy. Though children are not a requisite for every marriage, this is the community intended by God for their procreation and nurture in life and faith.

It is the nature of the human condition that we sometimes fail to sustain lifelong vows or to grow in love and caring for the other. We are offered God's forgiveness, the promise of a new beginning, and the resources for future flourishing. Prevailing cultural individualism has eroded confidence in and commitment to the institution of marriage. This can be overcome in part by supporting the public nature of marriage, in both church and society, that seeks to protect and preserve the interests of all; and by teaching the values and skills that assist persons in making and sustaining commitments.

REFLECTION

Several members of the Commission remarked that David's description of matrimony as understood by the church does not meet today's realities. For example:

+ Matrimony is described as the union of a man and a woman. Many Christians, including Anglicans, are struggling how to describe the desire of two men or two women to commit themselves to each other before God.
+ Failure to sustain lifelong vows is mentioned, but the word "divorce" is not used. The church's changing attitude over time towards divorce should be presented.
+ Does God intend children to be born into a *marriage* relationship, not merely into a loving and supportive relationship? The latter is becoming increasingly common in Canada and elsewhere.

ORDERED MINISTRY

Walter Deller

Anglicans maintain a tradition of three orders of ministry: bishops, priests, and deacons. For many years the diaconate has been regarded in practice as a transitional stage on the way to priesthood, but parts of the Anglican world are again exploring it as a permanent order. The argument for a threefold ministry seems clear until we consider that at the Reformation a sizeable portion of the Western world, reading the Scriptures equally diligently, dispensed with some or all of the threefold orders.

It seems to me, however, that ordination is a sacrament of the church because it manifests to us, in an outward and visible sign, the orderly outpouring of God's grace. All baptized people are called, at some time in their daily life and work, to "oversight" (*episcope*), to "gathering, feeding, proclaiming and eldering" (*presbyteros*), and to "service" (*diakonia*). In a sacramental and iconic sense, those persons the church calls and orders remind us of how these essential works are to be shaped uniquely by the imprint of Christ's life, death, and resurrection.

Some of the questions and tensions about orders that continue to perplex the church are these:

+ Does the worthiness of the individual minister affect the efficacy of his/her ministration?
+ Must a bishop or a priest preside at the eucharist in all circumstances? If so, why do we permit anyone to baptize in an emergency?

✦ How do we find a balance between understanding ordered ministry as functional (being responsible for certain ecclesial acts) and ontological (the very being of the minister is identified as "ordered")? These and other questions relating to ordered ministry will be discussed in book four.

ANOINTING

David Reed and Laverne Jacobs

Unction anointing, in the BCP [320], is the act of administering oil (usually olive oil) to a person receiving prayers for healing. It is administered on the forehead and/or the hands. It was an apt symbol in Mediterranean culture, in which oil was plentiful and frequently used for medicinal purposes [see Luke 10:34]. In the Bible it was used symbolically in a variety of public acts, including the crowning of kings and consecrations to God's service.

In the New Testament in particular, anointing with oil was part of the ministry of healing, sometimes accompanied by the laying on of hands [see Mark 6:13, James 5:14–15]. It has continued in the church's ministry as a symbol of God's effectual presence and purpose. It is in this sense that anointing is often regarded as a sacramental sign of God's presence and power to heal.

In the Anglican tradition oil for unction is blessed by the bishop and administered by priests and "lay anointers" as a sign of the church's identification with the sick person. In Native churches, healing is an important ministry, due in part to a holistic understanding of creation, so that reconciliation with God must include the emotional and physical dimensions as well as the spiritual. Anointing with oil is a potent sign of the sacred, the powerful presence of a healing God.

NOURISHED BY GRACE

Prayer

REQUESTS

I asked for Peace —
    My sins arose,
    And bound me close,
I could not find release.

I asked for Truth —
    My doubts came in,
    And with their din
They wearied all my youth.

I asked for Love —
    My lovers failed,
    And griefs assailed
Around, beneath, above.

I asked for Thee,
    And Thou didst come
    To take me home
Within Thy heart to be.

Digby Mackworth Dolben (1848–1867)

The modern tendency towards individual expression requires recovering a balance between individual and corporate prayer. In particular we must avoid imposing any individual's private experience on the corporate body.

VICTORIA MATTHEWS

In recent years a frequently articulated concern accompanying the proliferation of service books, translations of the Bible, and even hymn collections is that we have lost both our understanding and commitment to common prayer. Gone are the days when one could attend an Anglican church anywhere and feel at home. I am convinced that we are being challenged to deepen our understanding of public and private prayer and their relationship one to another.

Thirty years ago [1971] the National Executive Council of the General Synod resolved

> That in future revisions of our Common Prayer Book, more emphasis be given to permissive forms and less to mandatory forms of worship, in order that in the use of one common book, we may still achieve that flexibility and variety we deem desirable. And that in the meantime General Synod be asked to give guidance to diocesan authorities in relaxing the rigid conformist notes still written into our Common Prayer Book [*BAS*, Introduction, 7].

Parallel to the publication of the *Book of Alternative Services,* the supplementary *Eucharistic Prayers, Services of the Word, and Night Prayer,* and such daily service books as *Celebrating Common Prayer* [1992], there has been a growing interest in specialized or focused spiritualities. One can read books and take courses exploring Celtic spirituality, creation spirituality, Native spirituality, feminist spirituality, Benedictine spirituality — the list goes on. The result has been a renewed interest and commitment to spiritual direction and also an increased focus on private prayer and meditation. Where in all this are we to find the right balance and relation of private and public prayer?

It is very clear from the New Testament that Jesus both went apart to pray alone [see Luke 4:1ff.; 4:42; 9:18; 11:1] and participated in public worship [see Luke 4:16; 4:33; 20:1], and it can be argued that in Jesus' life there is a recognizable rhythm between the two. Synagogue and Temple worship drew the community together in worship and teaching. When Jesus went apart to a deserted place, he was seeking strength for the trials of his life. Neither private nor public prayer is understood as sufficient of itself; each needs the other. Jesus taught about both private prayer [see Matthew 6:5ff.] and corporate prayer [see Matthew 6: 9–13].

Opinion about faith and the practice of prayer has continuously changed over the centuries. Whereas at various times in history the very thought of privatized faith or religion would have seemed absurd, for the past fifty years or more the personal relationship of the Christian with God has, for many, been paramount. In Anglican circles we hear this attitude in phrases such as, "making my communion," "Who is Jesus for you?" and "That's not the God I worship and pray to." The notion, "true to you" — a hallmark of the post-modern era — has led Anglicans and many others into customized religious observance.

It takes many forms. One example is a married couple who had attended their urban parish for decades and greatly loved the liturgy, preaching, and community. They wouldn't willingly have missed Sunday worship there. Nevertheless, when on several occasions they lived abroad for six months or a year, they didn't darken the door of any church because it wasn't St. Philip's. On a broader scale, there are Anglicans who avoid *BAS* worship and others who decline Prayer Book worship and still others who declare the supplementary prayers unacceptable. Again we return to the question: What constitutes common and public prayer and where is it found in our Anglican church?

Within Anglicanism it was Richard Hooker who established that the corporate prayer of the church and the prayer of individual Christians are two distinct entities [Wright, 16]. Common and public prayer have long been understood to hold up "a standard of faith and practice, impressing on both minister and people, at every performance of public worship, the important doctrines and duties of the Gospel" [**John Henry Hobart**, *A Companion for the Book of Common Prayer* quoted in Wright, 95]. The intent and effect is to bring those assembled into common

understanding, commitment, and devotion. The celebration of the Holy Eucharist, the absolution of sins, and the blessing of the people are furthermore the offering of a priestly ministry that is both common and public.

The present challenge is to overcome the heightened expectations of having one's personal preferences met, and to return to common prayer. Common prayer must be Trinitarian, sacramental, and devotional, but the forms it takes naturally differ across time and space. For example, fifty years ago Anglican worship around the globe would have been almost certainly in English. Now every diocese in Canada, let alone every province in the Anglican Communion, has celebrations of the eucharist in diverse languages.

However, when diversity in public celebration means a eucharistic prayer composed by a member of the local community, the notion of common prayer is betrayed. And much more so when the sentiment is expressed or implied, "This is who *I* am; this is *my* theology." Only those well versed in Christian devotion, whose lives bear fruit for the well-being of the

---

RICHARD HOOKER (CA 1554–1600) was the most important theologian of the English Reformation and one of the greatest of Anglican theologians. He argued forcibly against the literal interpretation of Scripture and for the use of reason in theology. He is remembered for his monumental work, *Treatise on the Laws of Ecclesiastical Polity,* which argues for a foundation of natural law that "is the expression of God's supreme reason" [*ODCC,* 789]. Hooker saw the church as dynamic and, consequently, its polity can rightly be adapted to changing circumstances.

JOHN HENRY HOBART (1775–1830) was Bishop of New York (1816–1830) and founder of The General Theological Seminary (1817) in Chelsea, Manhattan. He wrote *A Companion to the Book of Common Prayer* and *A Companion for the Festivals and Feasts of the Protestant Episcopal Church.*

community, are suited for the crafting of public liturgy, and the result must be acceptable to the whole community of the church.

The Book of Revelation portrays heaven as an assembly of worship. There is no obvious common rite, but there is harmony, and the focus is clearly God and the adoration of the Holy Trinity. The Anglican Church of Canada has continued that focus as we join our voices with those of the heavenly host. I do not experience disconnection with that heavenly act of worship when the gathered community I join uses the Prayer Book, the *BAS*, or the supplementary prayers approved by General Synod in 1998. I rejoice in the diversity, and I am also keenly aware of the commonality that underlies them.

Prayer unites the soul to God, for though the soul may be always like God in nature and in substance restored by grace, it is often unlike him in condition through sin on man's part. Then prayer is a witness that the soul wills as God wills, and it eases the conscience and fits man to grace. And so he teaches us to pray and to have firm trust that we shall have it; for he holds us in love, and wants to make us partners in his good will and work. And so he moves us to pray for what it pleases him to do.

From *Showings* by Julian of Norwich.
Translated by Edmund Colledge and James Walsh.

Mysticism, the quest for direct and intimate union with God, is the goal and summit of all religious life. Its development is continuous throughout Christian history, and it has featured strongly in Anglican tradition.

ROBERT CROUSE

Mysticism is the quest for and the possession of a direct and intimate union of the soul with God in loving contemplation, and thus it is the goal and summit of all religious life. **William James** quotes St. Paul in his lectures, *The Varieties of Religious Experience*: "I live, yet not I, but Christ liveth in me" [Galatians 2:20] and goes on to remark:

> This overcoming of all the usual barriers between the individual and the Absolute is the great mystic achievement. In mystic states we both become one with the Absolute and we become aware of our oneness. This is the everlasting and triumphant mystical tradition, hardly altered by differences in clime or creed .... so that there is about mystical utterances an eternal unanimity.... Perpetually telling of the unity of men with God, their speech ante-dates languages, and they do not grow old [419].

In its historical development, Christian mysticism certainly drew upon various religious traditions, but it found its essential nutriment in the canonical Scriptures, especially the Song of Songs in the Old Testament and the Revelation of St. John the Divine in the New, and such other New Testament passages as St. Paul's account of his ecstatic vision [2 Corinthians 12] and Jesus' High Priestly Prayer [John 17].

In the thought of the church Fathers, mysticism was given its particular Christian shape in relation to the central Christian doctrines of the Trinity and the Incarnation. Thus, union with God could not be understood as only intellectual (the Word) or as only a union of love (the Spirit), but as a union at once, and equally, in knowledge and love. The Incarnate Word, with his bestowal of the Spirit, was seen as the way of the soul's ascent to that union, to be attained perhaps fleetingly in this life but fully ("face to

---

THOMAS AQUINAS (CA 1225–1274), a Dominican philosopher and theologian, was the best known of the medieval schoolmen ("scholastics"). He was strongly influenced by Aristotle, whose writings had only recently become known in the West, and he was largely responsible for moving philosophy and theology away from the Neoplatonism that had characterized it from at least the time of Augustine, although Aquinas passed on much of Augustinian thought. Aquinas's writings were extensive and covered the range of theology. He is best known for his *Summa Theologica,* which originated in lectures to university students. His theology was marked by a sharp distinction between the natural and the supernatural, and between reason and faith. From 1879 until recently his philosophy and theology (known as "thomism") was the official teaching of the Roman Catholic Church. Aquinas has been influential also in Anglicanism. Not only was Richard Hooker fully versed in Thomism, but recent Anglican theologians (for example, E.L. Mascall) have followed him.

WILLIAM JAMES (1842–1910) was an American philosopher, psychologist, and educator. His most famous work is *The Varieties of Religious Experience* [1902] in which he analyzed "conversion" and introduced the language of "once born" and "twice born" applied to religious types. He taught that there is no certain proof of the existence of God, but that belief in God is legitimate and beneficial.

face") in heaven. Understood in that way, mysticism was not an optional "extra" but the very essence of Christian life.

It was that perspective, inherited by the Middle Ages, that shaped the piety of medieval Christendom. The ancient Christian understanding of liturgy as mystery was enhanced by emphasis upon the dramatic representation of the mystery of faith as the occasion for the worshippers' awe-filled anticipation of the mystical union. **Thomas Aquinas** wrote:

> Both flesh and spirit at thy presence fail,
> Yet here thy presence we devoutly hail.

The very buildings of Christian worship were designed with that mystical conception of liturgy in mind.

The monasteries of medieval Europe were the centres where the theory and practice of mysti-cal piety developed, and since virtually all medieval theologians were monks, nuns, or friars, the history of medieval mysticism is the history of medieval theology. But the elaborate refinement of the theory and practice of mystical piety in the religious houses of the late Middle Ages had the effect of isolating mysticism as a very special vocation. It was marked by an increasing tendency to separate mysticism from scholasticism and feeling from thought, and it fostered a mysticism of the Spirit divorced from the Word, a piety of the heart and not of the mind.

In general, the Protestant Reformation was unsympathetic towards this affective piety, which sometimes seemed to suggest a heavenly reward for human merit. But **Luther** himself valued highly a fifteenth-century mystical work called *Theologia Germanica*. When later Lutheranism inclined towards scholasticism, mystical piety was revived among the **German Pietists**. A key

---

MARTIN LUTHER (1483–1546) was a German monk and scholar whose conviction that the church needed reform led him to oppose papal authority and some doctrines that he associated with it. 31 October, 1517, when Luther affixed a collection of ninety-five theses to the door of the castle church in the university city of Wittenburg, is usually taken as the overt beginning of the Protestant Reformation. Luther's central teaching was "justification by faith alone." Luther also taught "the bondage of the will" to sin, that is, the human will is not free to choose good (a doctrine inherited from Augustine). Therefore the Christian is justified by the work of Christ without cooperation on his or her part. Justification does not make a Christian righteous, but "imputes" or ascribes righteousness in the sight of God.

GERMAN PIETISM began in the Lutheran Church in the seventeenth century as a reaction against what was seen to be a dogmatic and dry formalism into which the church had fallen. The movement condemned the use of philosophy and theology in teaching and preaching, wanting them to be replaced by devotional meetings only. The University of Halle was a centre of the movement for many years. Pietism had many forms — one emphasizing penance, grace, and rebirth, another personal devotion to Christ as Redeemer. Its influence persisted and spread outside Germany. Wesleyan Methodism has much in common with it.

figure in that revival was **Jakob Boehme**, who in turn exercised a dominant influence on William Law, the greatest English devotional writer of the eighteenth century. His *A Serious Call to a Devout and Holy Life* (1729) influenced many, among them John and **Charles Wesley.**

Anglican theologians of the Post-Reformation era were open to the mystical traditions of the Middle Ages, and also to the mystical teachings of French and Spanish Roman Catholics. There was not among these Anglicans any suggestion that mysticism was a special vocation; it was seen simply as the deepest dimension of the ordinary life of the Christian soul growing in the knowledge and love of God. The great Puritan divine, Richard Baxter, exhorts his parishioners to continual meditation on the joys of heaven. The great medieval works of mystical devotion never ceased to be read by Anglican divines of various persuasions. John Wesley, for example, edited **Thomas à Kempis** *The Imitation of Christ* for the use of his followers. The leaders of the **Tractarian Movement** also drew on Continental Roman Catholic mystical literature, and it is perhaps to **Edward Pusey** more than any other, that modern Anglicanism owes it recognition of the mystical traditions of Christian piety.

In the early decades of the twentieth-century

Anglican theologians made important contributions to the study of mysticism. *Mysticism* by Evelyn Underhill (1875–1941, a well-known English writer on mysticism and spiritual director) and *Vision of God* by Kenneth Kirk (1886–1954, Bishop of Oxford, and much respected moral theologian and spiritual writer) have become classics. More recently, however, interest seems to have waned and mysticism appears to have become foreign and irrelevant. Are Anglicans no longer interested in that intimate union with God in knowledge and love, which is the substance of Christian mysticism? Are there modern substitutes? Does contemporary religion have different goals?

THOMAS À KEMPIS (CA 1380–1471) was a German ascetical writer who is thought to be the author of the enormously popular *The Imitation of Christ.* He lived most of his life as a religious in the community of the Canons Regular/Augustinian Canons. *The Imitation of Christ* is a manual of spiritual devotion that, as its title suggests, teaches that the way to perfection is to follow Christ as a model.

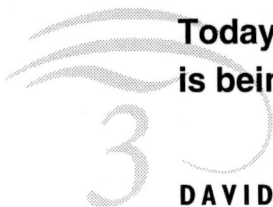

Today Christian spirituality of all mystical resemblance is being explored across all traditions.

DAVID REED

Mysticism is making a comeback! The 200-year long arm of the **Enlightenment** is withering. Protests against rationalism have persisted from **Romanticism** to the **New Age Movement** (please see page 50). Mysticism has a much longer history, spanning world religions, nature religions, and individual spirituality. It is highly experiential, often claiming a direct unmediated contact with the divine that is "ineffable" or incommunicable to others.

Mystical faith has been part of Christianity from earliest days including, as some claim, Paul and John from the New Testament period, early theologians such as Augustine, and much of Eastern Orthodoxy. It flourished in medieval Christianity but was discouraged by the Protestant Reformers as a deviation from biblical faith, though elements of mystical devotion appear in Luther. Phenomena similar to mysticism occurred in the emotional conversion experiences that accompanied the mass revivalistic movement of the eighteenth-century **Great Awakening**. One can trace the influence of the seventeenth-century French mystics, **François Fenelon** and **Madame Guyon,** on the evangelical "Higher Life" of the nineteenth century, a movement centred in the British **Keswick Conventions.** A prolific writer and ardent evangelical proponent of mystical faith in this century was **A. W. Tozer**. Today Christian spirituality of

---

ENLIGHTENMENT is the term applied to the period of European history usually considered to extend from the late seventeenth until the end of the eighteenth century. In philosophy and science, it tended to take the view that relying on faith as a means of drawing conclusions about the nature of the world and the human place in the world had led to the destructive wars fought over religion throughout Europe during the previous centuries. Instead, it emphasized the use of sensory observation and logical deduction and induction — that is, reason — to draw conclusions. These conclusions, they claimed, would be free from the perspectives or biases implied by faith and doctrinal statements.

ROMANTICISM had a resurgence in the nineteenth century as a pendulum swing against what was seen by many as the over-rationalism of the eighteenth century. Romanticism is not systematized, but reflects rather a temperament or attitude (see Jane Austen, *Sense and Sensibility*). It usually prefers emotion to reason and imagination to "fact." The best-known English romantic poets were Coleridge, Shelley, and Keats, with many less talented followers. Romanticism is reflected in the church in certain music, art, and architecture — particularly, although not exclusively, that of the Victorian period.

THE GREAT AWAKENING was an American Christian revival movement of the mid-eighteenth century marked by extreme emotionalism. Although its leaders, Jonathan Edwards and George Whitefield, discouraged excess, the Massachussets government forbade unauthorized itinerant preaching. Visible evidence of spiritual rebirth was expected to be the mark of every Christian; those who did not evince such were thought not to be saved.

THE KESWICK MOVEMENT is an evangelical movement, sometimes called "The Higher Life Movement," which emerged in England in the 1870s, with an emphasis on personal holiness. Following a series of conferences led by visiting American scholars, a convention was held at Keswick (in the Lake District). The conventions continue there to the present day. A distinctive teaching on sanctification is that sin, though not eradicated, can be made ineffectual in the believer's life. One of the leading promoters of Keswick spirituality within Anglican circles was the Bishop of Durham, Handley H.C. Moule.

mystical resemblance is being explored across all traditions, from the creation spirituality of **Matthew Fox** to the Pentecostal-charismatic movement.

But for some Christians, mysticism is problematic. It appears to share many common characteristics with the spiritual experience of other religions, such as an encounter with the Divine by direct intuition, the sense of being intimately united with the Ground or Source of all being, a tendency to regard the mystical experience as revelatory and definitive, and the frequent accompaniment of unusual physical phenomena (visions, voices, falling, shaking).

These commonalities are less likely to be signals of an encounter with Ultimate Truth than indicators of a natural human capacity for self-transcendence that can be activated by God or natural stimuli. That is, the test of authenticity cannot be located within the experience itself. For Christians, Anglicans in particular, the authority for discernment is mediated through Scripture, with the guidance of the church's tradition and reason.

With few exceptions, Christian mystics have consistently described their experience as an encounter with the risen Christ, not the incomprehensible and unknowable One.

FRANÇOIS DE SALIGNAC DE LA MOTHE FENELON (1651–1715), Archbishop of Cambrai, and **MME JEANNE MARIE BOUVIER DE LA MOTHE GUYON (1648–1717)** were influential spiritual figures in sixteenth-seventeenth-century France. They — particularly Mme Guyon — are remembered for their promotion of a type of spirituality that is intensively negative to human effort, teaching complete passivity before God and the annihilation of the will. Once this state is reached, by means of non-discursive objectless meditation, the person is flooded by divine light, becomes incapable of sin, and need not, indeed must not, be distracted by the usual activities of Christian life — acts of faith, prayer, and good works. This teaching earned the name "Quietism" or "Illuminism," and was viewed with great suspicion by religious authorities, notably Jacques Benigne Bossuet (1627–1704), Bishop of Meaux. Several of Mme Guyon's positions were condemned at Issy in 1695. A heated controversy between Fenelon and Bossuet followed, and some of Fenelon's teachings were condemned in 1699. Fenelon is also remembered for his pastoral generosity and his defence of the church against Jansenism.

A.W. TOZER (1897–1963) was an American-born evangelical pastor and author who is best known for his writings on prayer and the spiritual life. He was often critical of the superficiality of Protestant spirituality and frequently drew upon the medieval mystical tradition. His lifelong ministry was with The Christian and Missionary Alliance, serving for over a decade as editor of the *Alliance Weekly*. Before his death he was pastor of Avenue Road Church in Toronto. One of his most popular books is *The Pursuit of God*.

MATTHEW FOX is a spiritual theologian popular for his distinctive theology of creation spirituality. A former Roman Catholic priest and Dominican, he was received as a priest into the Episcopal Church after being censured by the Vatican. He teaches that all creation is good, but that the traditional teaching of the Fall distorts this "original blessing" as taught in the Bible. His theology of creation blends Christian spirituality with the mystical tradition, global Indigenous spiritualities, new scientific insights, and art. *Original Blessing* is one of the most popular of his twenty-four books. He is founder and president of University of Creation Spirituality in Oakland, California.

Neither their experience nor writings give cause for reducing Christianity to a spoke in the great wheel of world religions. The familiar language of "in Christ," "union with Christ," and "filled with the Spirit" bespeaks a faith that is not confined to mental assent or codes of behaviour, but breathes the faith of Scripture and the church with the intimacy of a lover.

New Age Movement is the name popularly given to a loosely networked movement that emerged in North America in the late 1960s. The term "New Age" refers to the astrological claim that the world is entering the Age of Aquarius, an era of global peace and harmony. NAM's (New Age Movement) appearance came as a surprise to many religion watchers whose attention at the time was focused on secularism.

NAM is not entirely novel but belongs to an older stream of spirituality that combines mystical experience with a scientific understanding of nature as energy, and the capacity of persons to be enlightened and transformed by that energy. But the NAM version of metaphysical and occult religion was shaped by certain cultural influences. A change in American immigration policy in the 1960s produced an influx of immigrants from Asian countries, people who brought Eastern religious teachings and practices, especially from Buddhism and Hinduism. Environmentalists were attracted to Eastern ideas of the close relationship between spiritual energy and nature. This was occurring at a time when the popular culture of individualism was beginning to produce negative attitudes towards society's institutions, resulting in a turning away from institutional religion. Finally, NAM has shown itself to be highly adaptive in the way it connects Eastern spirituality with current Western scientific ideas and popular humanistic psychologies.

NAM cannot be defined by a unified core philosophy. It is more a network of people with varied interests. But there are discernible commonalities. First, the heart of *the universe is mystically One* (monism) in a way that incorporates the human and natural world in the divine. God is not qualitatively different from creation but is the force that embraces and infuses it. Humans, therefore, have the potential to cooperate with the universal Spirit as divine beings.

Fundamental to NAM is the all-encompassing vision of a *radical transformation of the world*, individuals, and the cosmos. The world's deep problem to be overcome is illusion, ignorance of the true nature of things. The source of the needed transformation is *universal energy*, known by various names — ch'i, mana, mind, odic force, prana, spirit.

What is required is enlightenment and the right means of gaining access to the healing powers of the universe. These means may be meditation (getting in touch with one's divinity), mediums (clairvoyants, channelers, shamans, extra-terrestrial spirit guides), chakras (energy centres in the human body where the universal energy can be received), crystals (stones with powers to cure and enhance life), or horoscopes and tarot cards.

NAM vision is a utopian world of peace and harmony, a world that is attainable through the universal energy of love. NAM rejects the "dogmatism" of institutional religion, and envisions a time when the world's faiths will become one. After three decades NAM is no longer a movement because many of its ideas and practices are now embedded in mainstream culture, and are even embraced by an increasing number of practising Christians.

The long tradition of Christian pilgrimage, deriving from biblical precedents, is a metaphor for the "journey" on the Christian way.

JOANNE McWILLIAM

He who would valiant be
   Gainst all disaster,
   Let him in constancy
   Follow the Master.

There's no discouragement
   Shall make him once relent
   His first avowed intent
   To be a pilgrim.

John Bunyan (1628–1688)

A pilgrim is a very special kind of traveller, found in all the major world religions. She or he undertakes a long, often difficult, journey — both geographical and spiritual — to a sacred place. Sometimes the journey is taken to fulfil a vow, sometimes from other religious motives. The place may be considered sacred because of someone who lived there (the Holy Land, Medina), because there has been a special revelation there (Sinai, Xarnath), because a holy person is buried there (Compostela, Canterbury), or because a holy thing is associated with it (Walsingham).

Christian shrines and pilgrimages were first encouraged to honour the martyrs and later to counter pagan holy places. The **Venerable Bede** tells us in *The History of the English Church and People*, ch. 30, that Christians often appropriated springs, mountains, and other natural features that the pagans revered and gave them a Christian significance. The church of San Clemente in Rome is an outstanding example. The emotions evoked by the aura of sanctity surrounding the special geographical location stimulate the imagination and foster faith and devotion. "To the Christian mind, the saints were both present with God in spirit and present on earth in their physical remains" [Taylor, 324]. The place of pilgrimage, therefore, is a place where the material and spiritual worlds meet, and it has something of a sacramental nature.

While the sacred place is associated with spiritual or physical healing, it often gains in wealth and prestige as well. For this reason, early and medieval bishops encouraged local shrines, but on the other hand, local shrines were feared by the papacy as being centrifugal. To counter the trend towards local shrines, Rome — already a place of pilgrimage because both Peter and Paul are buried there — was promoted even more as the site of the papal presence.

In Old Testament times the Temple, in which the Ark of the Covenant was housed, was the most important focus of pilgrimage. "I was glad when they said to me, 'Let us go to the house of the Lord.'" [Psalm 122:1]. Its importance is reflected throughout the whole of Psalm 122 and the other Psalms of Ascent. Every Jewish man was expected to journey to Jerusalem once a year, and

> **BEDE THE VENERABLE (673–735)** was a monk in Northumbria, England, first at the monastery of Wearmouth and then at Jarrow. He was probably the most learned person in England at that time. Bede made a special study of scripture and published several commentaries, considered to be his best works. His writings, totalling at least thirty, covered other areas as well. Although a follower of Augustine, Bede went beyond him to teach that God works also outside the church. He was an early exponent of what is today called "inculturation." Bede is best remembered, however, for his work, *A History of the English Church and People*, which has earned him the title "the father of English history." His tomb in Durham cathedral is still a place of pilgrimage.

the Fourth Gospel depicts Jesus going there frequently [see 2:13, 10:22, 12:12ff]. But there were other pilgrimage sites: Bethel, for example, where the Lord wrestled with Jacob on a ladder stretching from heaven to earth [see Genesis 28:10-22].

When Christian pilgrimages to the Holy Land began is disputed, but they were certainly being undertaken by the fourth century. The travel diary of a Spanish woman named Egeria survives, and from it we know a good deal about the conditions of travel, the hospitality offered, and the places visited, as well as the liturgy of Holy Week there. Pilgrimages to Palestine became particularly popular after Helena, mother of the Emperor Constantine, claimed to have found fragments of Christ's cross there.

The Protestant Reformers discouraged pilgrimages, seeing them (wrongly) as unbiblical. But they could not wipe them out altogether, and the journey of the Puritans to New England had some of the characteristics of a pilgrimage. That pilgrimages lent themselves to trivialization (*The Canterbury Tales*) or abuse (the Crusades) is evident. Nevertheless they were and remain vibrant expressions of real devotion.

The long and difficult physical journey of pilgrimage has been understood to have a spiritual parallel. Christian life has always been seen as a journey or a way, and pilgrimage becomes a metaphor for it (for example, **John Bunyan**, *Pilgrim's Progress*). It has been said that we are "resident aliens." This sentiment is found also in the great Welsh hymn, "Guide me, O thou great Jehovah, pilgrim through this barren land." But both these expressions, although containing something of truth — that we are made for God and restless until we rest in God — are excessive. We are not aliens, this is *our* world; we love it and have responsibilities towards it. But it is not our *only* world; we look forward to another. As the Letter to the Hebrews says,

[Those who say they are pilgrims] have acknowledged that they are strangers and exiles on earth. For people who speak thus make it clear that they are seeking a homeland.... They desire a better country, that is a heavenly one [Hebrews 11:13-16a].

JOHN BUNYAN AND PILGRIM'S PROGRESS.
BUNYAN (1628–1688) was a tradesman who is thought to have learned how to read and write by reading the Bible. He sided with Parliament during the Civil War and by 1657 was a recognized preacher in the Congregational Church. Bunyan was imprisoned at the Restoration and wrote several of his works in prison. His most famous work, a classic of Christian literature, was

Pilgrim's Progress, first written in 1676; a second, expanded edition appeared in 1678. Simply written, the book offered religious language that became well known to the English-speaking religious world, and beyond: "the City of Destruction," "the Hill of Difficulty," "the Slough of Despair," "the House Beautiful," and the words often spoken at funerals, "All the trumpets sounded for him on the other side."

The high calling of Christian life is to live every day in the way of Christ, and the experience of pilgrimage enables a person to discover sacred meaning in the most mundane and inconsequential of daily events.

A number of years ago the Reverend Ben Lochridge of Lorne Park, Mississauga, spent part of his sabbatical leave walking the ancient pilgrimage route to **Santiago de Compostela**. As his neighbour and bishop, I was fascinated by his stories of this adventure of the spirit. Imagine the third most important pilgrimage site in the Christian world, and a route that has been traveled for a thousand years. Bitten by the bug of curiosity and knowing I enjoyed distance walking, I headed off to Spain that summer. There was time to walk only the last one hundred and fifty kilometers, but it was enough to make me eager to return. To date, I have walked the entire Franciscan Way (eight hundred kilometers) twice, although never all at one time.

Each pilgrimage is unique and teaches new things. Kurt Vonnegut, Jr. (a highly regarded American novelist, b. 1922) had it right when he said, "Strange travel suggestions are dancing lessons from God." Yet in my experience every pilgrimage is life transforming.

The word "pilgrim" is from the Latin *per agrum* (through the field). It reminds us that we live out our lives on sacred ground, and it invites us to recall that we are part of creation, created to love and serve the God who made us.

I suppose going on a pilgrimage could be little more than a variation of what is called "the geographic cure" — we travel or change our fixed address in hope of escaping our present reality. We set out, not like Abram and Sarai out of obedience to God, but in the desperate hope that a new beginning will erase the past and offer new freedom. True pilgrimage is different. It is undertaking a sacred journey in prayer. It is waiting on God. Far from taking control of one's future, pilgrimage entails consciously putting oneself in the hands of God and living each day in faith.

Pilgrimage therefore is a symbol of the Christian life. Indeed, if one sets out for Canterbury, Jerusalem, or Compostela, the climax of the journey is not arriving but recognizing that the destination is not what one thought it was. The real destination is eternal life. Thus, one's return home after the official pilgrimage is really a matter of recognizing that everyday life is a pilgrimage lived out before God. **Robert Louis Stevenson** expressed this beautifully in "A Christmas Sermon."

SANTIAGO DE COMPOSTELA is a city in northwest Spain where St. James the Great, the Apostle, is said to be buried. From the eleventh century it became a national and religious centre for the fight against the Moors who had invaded Spain. Today it is famous as a shrine, attracting thousands of pilgrims a year.

ROBERT LOUIS STEVENSON (1850–1994) was a Scots writer who, despite poor health, wrote prolifically. His work covered many genres. He is remembered for his poetry (*A Child's Garden of Verses*), for his adventure stories (*Kidnapped, Treasure Island*), his travel stories (*Travels on a Donkey*), and general fiction (*The Strange Case of Doctor Jekyll and Mr Hyde*). Although he was tremendously popular during his lifetime, there was a critical reaction in the early twentieth century, but his stories and his poetry for children are still widely read.

PILGRIMAGE Victoria Matthews   53

We require higher tasks, because we do not recognize the height of those we have. Trying to be kind and honest seems an affair too simple and too inconsequential for gentlemen of our heroic mould; we have rather set ourselves to something bold, arduous and conclusive; we had rather found a schism or suppress a heresy, cut off a hand or mortify an appetite. But the task before us ... is rather one of microscopic fineness, and the heroism required is that of patience. There is no cutting of the Gordian knots of life; each must be smilingly unraveled.

The high calling is everyday life, and the experience of pilgrimage seems dedicated to convincing the pilgrim that meaning is found in the most mundane and inconsequential daily events. The walk to Compostela is a series of single steps. There are very, very few necessities for the journey: water, a bit of bread, and strong feet. Nights are spent in basic shelters, called *refugios*. One learns to delight in small things: the song of a bird, the smile of a child, the cheery greeting of a fellow pilgrim, and a bit of shade in which to pause and rest. The pressures and worries of everyday life fade. One begins to understand why the consumer-driven, overly-full life of the rest of the year leaves us feeling empty and hungry.

Another common experience for pilgrims are moments of awe. Gone is the domesticated church of home. Instead, a chance encounter, a quick prayer, a phrase or image that speaks directly to one's heart brings an encounter with the Other, the eternal and ultimate mystery. The lesson is not to return home wishing one could again be on the path, but to recognize that the God of surprises, the God of mystery, abides wherever life finds us. The voice of the Spirit speaks to those who have ears to hear. Attending the eucharist celebrated in the Basque language encouraged me to be particularly attentive to non-verbal communications. When the next pause in the journey allowed for a drink of water and a piece of bread broken from the daily loaf in my backpack, I became acutely aware that all life is a gift and that every meal is a sacramental refreshment of the moment.

God of pilgrims, strengthen our faith, we pray. Guide us through the uncertainties of our journey, and hold before us the vision of your eternal kingdom, made known to us in Jesus Christ our Lord.
[*BAS*, psalm prayer, 78].

Contemplation and action are complementary ways of responding to God's call and the needs of the world.

EILEEN SCULLY

There are times when it is tempting to want to feel secure, knowing that one is doing the right thing. When I was growing up in a fairly average Anglican parish, it occurred to me that praying properly meant using the right words.

When I was about ten, a family friend entered **The Sisterhood of Saint John the Divine**. I began to think of her as a professional "pray-er" and constructed fantasies of her peaceful life, away from the worries of the world, immersed in *real* prayer. At the same time in my life I remember being impressed by women in our parish who worked in the field of health care. From overhearing their conversation, I learned that their commitment to the marginalized, both in care and political activism, was deeply rooted in their Christian faith. Still, I harboured a sense that my friend, the SSJD sister, was leading a somehow more *holy* life than the others.

One of my earliest memories of the liturgy is of the two great commandments being read: "Hear, O Israel, ... thou shalt love the Lord the God with thy whole heart ....This is the first and greatest commandment. And the second is like unto it" (pause while the page is turned), "Thou shalt love thy neighbour as thyself." This raised a question, which it took me a long time to articulate: What could be the link between the two commandments, between — as it is classically articulated — contemplation and action?

It wasn't too long before I recognized that I had made caricatures for myself. I discovered that Sister Nonah was much engaged in both prayer and care for the sick, the poor, the marginalized. I began to notice the activists at prayer and realize that they tended the sanctuary as well. I became aware of the different gifts given to Christians.

"What must I do to be saved?" the lawyer asked Jesus, who responded by repeating the two great commandments. How easily we divide these loves and give priority to one or the other. The apparent rebuke to Martha for her busyness [Luke 10:38–42] follows the story of the Good Samaritan, and in the context of the whole chapter we cannot conclude that the contemplative role adopted by Mary is superior to service. To make a distinction between contemplation and action is to set up a false dichotomy; both are ways of paying attention to God's commandments.

When we are nurtured in prayer, and particularly by the common prayer that is the eucharist, we are shaped by God's promises and desires for us and the whole world. We attend to the vision of the reign of God where all will be welcomed

---

THE SISTERHOOD OF SAINT JOHN THE DIVINE is the only Anglican religious order for women founded in Canada (1884). Their rule is based on the Rule of Saint Benedict. The members' first and most important work is prayer (reflecting Benedict's *laborare est orare,* "to work is to pray"); they say the seven hours of the Divine Office daily. They are also active in corporal and spiritual works of mercy. The motherhouse is located in Willowdale, Ontario. The order has lay associates.

and there will be no mourning, suffering, death, injustice, hunger, or homelessness. That vision shapes the ways in which we attend to the needy in the world around us now, and that attention is not only activity, but is centred in a life animated by gratitude for God's love.

REFLECTION

+ Does the Anglican tradition of common prayer challenge the competitive individualism that pervades our society? What is the "glue" that holds together love of God and love of neighbour, prayer and politics, mystery and justice, study and play?

HOW THEN SHOULD WE LIVE?

KEY QUESTIONS

✦ What is the basis of Christian morality? What moral languages do we use?

✦ What obstacles do we encounter in our attempts to follow Christ?

✦ Do we understand salvation as an escape from the world or as a transformation of the world?

✦ Does Christian morality extend to concern for our social environment? Our earthly environment?

✦ How do we distinguish Christian living from cultural customs? Is healing part of the essential work of Christians?

At baptism Christians enter the life of the Spirit, a life variously described here by members of the Commission.

Commission members each wrote a short statement describing their understanding of Life in the Spirit.

Victoria Matthews

At holy baptism the new Christian is incorporated into the life of Christ and receives the Holy Spirit. Nothing is able to take away what is received in baptism. Nor is it possible for the Holy Spirit to "take over" the person's life so that he or she becomes captive and thereby loses freedom of action. Nevertheless, it is always possible that the baptized person will choose to cooperate with the grace received at baptism and lead a highly intentional life wherein the direction and guidance of the Holy Spirit is diligently sought. Such a life is lived in imitation of Christ.

What does such a life look like? Life in the Spirit is expressed in a daily life of prayer and study, in moral conduct, and in relationships at home, at work, and across the global village. The ability to forgive and accept forgiveness, generosity of spirit, and personal graciousness are evidence of the Spirit-led life.

The Epistle to the Galatians juxtaposes life in the Spirit with the desires of the flesh. Such a dichotomy doesn't sit easily with modern thought. Nevertheless, the fruits of the Spirit — love, joy, peace, patience, kindness, generosity, faithfulness, gentleness, and self-control [see Galatians 5:22] — are qualities enormously admired and desired by Christians and non-Christians alike. They might be described as attributes of someone who has achieved the fullest expression of what it is to be human. For Christians, life in the Spirit is nothing less than participation in the Risen Life of Christ and the Body of Christ on earth.

Edith Humphrey

We live in the Spirit because, like Jesus, we are "anointed" — we are little "c" Christs, led by the Spirit as "sons of God" [Romans 8:14]. Every Christian is led in the way of Christ — baptized to identify with Christ's death for the sins of the world, taken to the wilderness for testing and transformation, ordained into the ministry that announces God's new rule of peace, introduced into the joy of living and worshipping with God's people, drawn into suffering for Jesus' sake, and filled with the hope of resurrection and glory [see Romans 8:17].

Our call to the wilderness means that we invite the Spirit to correct and transform us, opening to the Spirit through confession, repentance, and attentive search for the will of Christ. Through the Spirit our lives and our words become the living declarations of God's presence, and we learn to love God's creation and people in his own way. We come to understand our priestly call to participate in the healing of the world, and to help nature give glory to the Lord. With Christ, we ache for a sad and sorrowing world, but also see its grandeur and its power to point to the Creator.

With others who have glimpsed the glory of God in the face of Jesus, we are drawn increasingly into the life of eucharist and worship. In all our work, prayer, joy, and life together, the Holy Spirit gives voice to what we can barely imagine, strengthens our weakness, and binds us together, across space, time, and human barriers, to become more fully the Body of Christ. Life in the Spirit means to see clearly who we now are and to anticipate in joy what we shall be when God is all in all.

David Reed

The bad news about "living in the Spirit" these days is that the term suffers from the Humpty Dumpty syndrome! It breaks up the Trinity, and confuses the Holy Spirit with the human spirit, which is easily reduced to emotions or self-promoting desires.

The good news is that to truly live in the Spirit is to experience the reversal of the shattered Humpty Dumpty. This turnabout begins in an encounter with Christ, the baptizer in the Spirit. His purpose is to empower his followers to be witnesses in the world. Spirit-baptism effects a deep conversion that creates a profound personal relationship with Christ and his company. It is not identical with water baptism, but seals the covenant of Christ's promise and invites us to share fully in his life.

Living in the Spirit means that our whole being is alive to Christ. This occurs in at least three ways. First, our life in Christ is made visible as the fruits of the Spirit are cultivated in us [see Galatians 5:22–23]. These are the qualities that describe and produce the *character of Christ*, and are not merely natural or cultural virtues.

Second, Christ is present through the *gifts* of the Spirit [see Romans 12:4–8; 1 Corinthians 12:4–11; Ephesians 4:11–12]. Our talents, skills, and intuitive insights become spiritual gifts when they are offered and transformed to accomplish God's purpose. They become in us the *ministry* of Christ, an *imitatio Christi*, through the Spirit's power.

Finally, the Spirit stirs our *affections* as we cry "Abba" ("dear Father") to the One whom Jesus calls God [see Romans 8:15]. This is not misguided mindless emotionalism. It is the motivation of the heart, yearning for God and being satisfied.

Joanne McWilliam

What does the phrase "life in the Spirit" mean? Some identify it with spirituality (a wider and often misused term). And some associate it with the rejection of the material world, especially our bodies. But this is not what "life in the Spirit" means. It means, rather, our sharing of the triune divine life. The Spirit is the Spirit of Christ, and both Spirit and Christ are one in being with God. We are taken up into the dynamic rhythm of the Three. "Life in the Spirit" is life in the resurrected Christ.

Christians enter this life by baptism. It is not merely a state, but also a journey and an adventure. We are strengthened in this journey into God by prayer and the sacraments, and by all that we do which transcends self for the sake of others, and which brings closer the Kingdom of God.

Laverne Jacobs

"You are all sons of God through faith in Christ Jesus for all of you who were baptized into Christ have clothed yourselves with Christ" [Galatians 3:26].

Through baptism I, as Anishnabe (a term, meaning "the people," which the Ojibwe use to describe themselves) have received the gift of the Spirit and the potential to be all that the Creator intends me to be. This gift is received within the context of my cultural identity. It does not negate my identity as Anishnabe, but rather transforms it and renews the gift of being a First Nations person: the sense of community, a particular worldview, long-suffering, respect, sharing, and valuing the gifts of others. Life in the Spirit then honours and embraces all the gifts the Creator has given me as Anishnabe. It means to be fully Anishnabe in Christ.

Eileen Scully

In baptism we are drawn by grace into the life, death, and resurrection of Christ, and into a new life in the Spirit. This life of the Spirit is a gift to the community of disciples: the gift of unity and healing and of life which holds, feeds, corrects, and guides us as we share in Christ's ministry of healing and reconciliation. It is a new thing: do we not perceive it [see Isaiah 43: 19]? In this life eyes are opened through grace to recognize the gifts given by God in creation and salvation. Ears are sensitized through grace to hear the cries of the sufferings of the world. Hearts are warmed through grace to embrace with healing love what is broken and in need.

Robert Crouse

Christian spiritual life is expressed in manifold ways.

> The wind bloweth where it listeth, and ye hear the sounds thereof, but ye cannot tell whence it cometh, or whither it goeth. So is everyone that is born of the Spirit [John 3:8].

Because we are finite, we possess a measure of the truth and a measure of the good, not in ourselves alone, but in a diversity of gifts and talents and vocations in the shared life of the community. St Paul makes that point when he compares the life of the church to the life of a body, to which every member makes a contribution [see 1 Corinthians 12]. Thus, life in the Spirit is life in that mutuality which we know as charity [see 1 Corinthians 13].

Our spiritual destiny lies in knowing and loving God — knowing as we are known and loving as we are loved. It is important that we keep that Trinitarian pattern, that interrelation of knowledge and love, that equality of Word and Spirit always before us. Always, the Word and the Spirit stand together, co-inhering and interpenetrating — the "experience" of the Spirit without the intelligible Word is amorphous and meaningless; the Word without the life-giving Spirit is dead. Thus, life in the Spirit means living in the knowledge and love of God, having the Word of God within our minds and hearts by the illuminating grace of God the Holy Spirit.

Anglican Christians agree that the Christian moral life is based on the Summary of the Law. And all Christians share common moral ground, both with each other and with non-Christians concerned to lead a moral life.

CHRISTOPHER LIND

The Christian life is a life lived. It is the practice of a "way of life." Indeed, early Christians were often called "people of the Way." Anglican Christians are people who have inherited a distinctive pattern of religious life. It includes worship but goes beyond debates about prayer books. The American Anglican theologian, Timothy Sedgewick, in his book, *The Christian Moral Life,* calls it the practice of piety. By this he means not the negative sense of being narrowly religious and judgemental, but rather the broader sense of being faithful, reverent, and just. Anglicans acknowledge God's presence in all aspects of life, so that the Christian life is not just a holy religion but also a wholly moral life.

For many Anglican Christians, the Ten Commandments are the foundation of the Christian life. The gospels of Matthew, Mark, and Luke record the story of people challenging Jesus to declare one commandment more important than the others. His response is to recite the summary of the Law from Deuteronomy.

> One of the scribes came near and heard them disputing with one another, and, seeing that he answered well, he asked him, "Which commandment is the first of all?" Jesus answered: The first is, "Hear, O Israel: the Lord our God, the Lord is One; you shall love your God with all your heart, and with all your soul, and with all your mind, and with all your strength." The second is this, "You shall love your neighbour as yourself. There is no other commandment greater than these." Then the scribe said to him:

> You are right, Teacher, you have truly said that "he is one, and beside Him there is no other"; and "to love him with all the heart, and with all the understanding, and with all the strength," and "to love one's neighbour as oneself"— this is much more important than all whole burnt offerings and sacrifices. When Jesus saw that he answered wisely, he said to him, "You are not far from the kingdom of God." After that, no one dared to ask him any question [Mark 12: 28–34].

In Deuteronomy the passage from which Jesus was quoting, continues:

> Keep these words that I am commanding you today in your heart. Recite them to your children and talk about them when you are at home, and when you are away, when you lie down and when you rise. Bind them as a sign on your hand, fix them as an emblem on your forehead, and write them on the doorposts of your house and on your gates [Deuteronomy 6: 6–9].

This is what Timothy Sedgewick means by the practice of piety. No part of life is untouched by this instruction. The Christian moral life involves love of God and love of neighbour. It involves heart, mind, soul, and strength. It is to be internalized by constant repetition at home and away. It is not a private practice but a public one, proclaimed from our doorposts and gates. And it is to be passed from generation to generation.

If we all agree that this is the foundation of our personal and common life, why is there so much disagreement about what is right? Let me try to explain.

A *moral life* is lived in conformity with one's understanding, knowledge, and experience of standards of goodness and rightness.

A *religious moral life* is lived in conformity with one's understanding, knowledge, and experience of the Divine. Different communities name the Divine in different ways — Allah, Vishnu, Buddha, God, the Unknowable, and the Unnamable. While specific moral directions may be different, the basic pattern is the same.

A *Christian moral life* is lived in conformity with one's understanding, knowledge, and experience of God in Christ. It is an active life in which one chooses to live a certain way. To adapt a well-known saying, "If living the Christian moral life were a crime, would there be enough evidence to convict you?"

Some Christians emphasize that, since Christianity is understandable by the application of reason informed by faith, moral life is a matter of reasoning through the complexities of every-day life, looking for the approach and *understanding* that will allow us to become the persons we were meant to be.

Some Christians emphasize that, since God is said to be revealed through the Scriptures, through the life of Jesus, and through nature, the moral life is a dedicated search for the *knowledge* that can be applied to everyday problems.

Some Christians emphasize that, since we all have the capacity to *experience* God, the moral life is a matter of seeking direct divine guidance for solutions to their moral dilemmas.

These differences in emphasis are one of the sources of conflict and misunderstanding among Christians on moral questions. Some people want to make a sharp distinction between the moral life of a Christian and the moral life of anyone else. However, since both Christians and non-Christians rely to a large extent on reason and wisdom, there is a significant area of common ground. It is possible, therefore, for Christians to make common cause on practical issues with anyone of good will, whether Christian or not.

The preoccupations of the modern world present challenges to both Christian discernment and discipleship.

EILEEN SCULLY

In the parish where I worship, I've noticed a change in the congregational *feeling* about renewal of baptismal vows. There seems to be a certain gusto in the responses. I think this has to do with an emerging consciousness of the *difference* of being a Christian in a secular world. We are all conscious of some kind of difference, but what is the difference in being "in the world but not of the world," which is where we are called by baptism? This is a question about discernment and discipleship.

Relationship with God is at the heart of the matter. God first calls us — in creation, in baptism, through the journeys of life and faith. Our response is praise born of gratitude, discernment of God's call, and willingness to follow where God leads us through Christ in the Spirit. Reaffirmation of baptismal vows reminds us in a powerful way of our identity — not so much a question of *who* we are, but of *whose* we are.

Discernment involves paying attention to who we are (through creation and grace) and to the careful stewardship of the gifts God gives us to respond to the call. This attentiveness requires clear vision to look both at ourselves and at the road ahead to see where God is calling us. Chris-

tian discernment is paying attention to the Spirit's activity in our lives, the life of the church, and the life of the world. John instructs us to "test the spirits if they be of God" [I John 4:1–6]. What, then, does it mean to be "of God"? This seems to be the lead-in question to 1 John 4:7–21, which begins, "Beloved, let us love one another, because love is from God; everyone who loves is born of God and knows God. Whoever does not love does not know God, for God is love." Christian discernment is awareness of God's love and its fruits in our lives. It also means acknowledging the sin that keeps us from attending fully to the Spirit's transformation of our hearts.

In a world that claims our attention to a thousand bits of information every minute, it can be hard to see through clearly to the world of the Spirit. In a competitive society, it can be hard to discover the path of the followers of Jesus. In a world crowded with many voices all claiming to be authoritative, it can be hard to identify and hear Jesus' voice.

Some mourn the church's loss of prominence and power in society, but wonderful energies are freed up when we're no longer concerned about maintaining them. The body that is the church

---

DIETRICH BONHOEFFER (1906–1945) was a German theologian who was executed for conspiring to overthrow the Nazi regime. In his *Letters and Papers from Prison* he advocated "religionless Christianity" for "a world come of age." He contrasted "religion," reliance on "cheap grace" from a supernatural source with "faith," trusting in the "costly grace" of disciples who share Christ's sufferings. Bonhoeffer urged his friend, Bishop George Bell of Chichester, not to be content with theological pronouncements, but to risk action in the struggle for world peace.

— and that is ourselves — starts to move, exercise its muscles, and unclog the arteries leading to the heart that is Christ. It stretches its legs, walks down the street, and acts as the Body of Christ is bound to act — reaching out to the marginalized, the poor, and the suffering; binding up wounds and drawing strangers together at the same table. Baptism into this body is baptism into a body in motion that is hearing God's call and responding to it.

The church as an institution has been pulled into litigation over residential schools. The desire for institutional self-protection produces fear that may obscure the call to discipleship.

Challenges like these are what make discipleship "costly," as **Dietrich Bonhoeffer** called it. The cost is paid in confronting what gets in the way of hearing Jesus and discerning what the gospel call to healing and reconciliation means now. Following Jesus means following the way of the cross to resurrection, and it is by following that we tell the gospel news to the church ("Go, tell the disciples ...") and the world ("Go, therefore and preach ...").

The deeper we get into reality, the more numerous will be the questions we cannot answer. For myself I cannot conceive truth, or rather, reality, as a geometrical figure of luminous lines, within which is sheer truth, and outside of which is sheer error; but I have to conceive such reality as light, in its centre blindingly luminous, having rings around it of lesser and lesser light, growing dimmer and dimmer until we are left in utter darkness.

Friederich von Hügel (1852–1925), *The Reality of God and Religion and Agnosticism.*

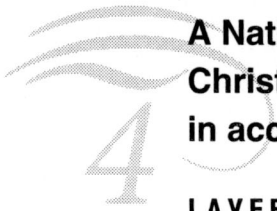

A Native Christian tells the story of the conflict he felt between his Christian faith and Native Spirituality. He shares his certainty that, in accepting both, he has entered into an authentic spirituality.

LAVERNE JACOBS

Christian Roots

On a memorable morning in May 1959, I "committed my life to Jesus Christ." Thus began a very convoluted spiritual journey.

This experience provided me with the stability and identity I needed as a Native youth growing up in the late 1950s and early 1960s. The social and economic conditions of my reserve community caused me tremendous shame. I struggled with all the stereotypes of the lazy drunken irresponsible Indian. As a new Christian, I gained a status that I did not enjoy as a Native person. I became a "child of God," an "heir of God and joint heir with Christ," and a "fellow citizen with the saints and members of the household of God" [see Romans 8:16–17;

Ephesians 2:19]. Following high school and a couple years in the work world, I entered an Anglican theological college.

During my seminary years I grew to appreciate the devotional life of the church. I learned about the church fathers and the history and traditions of the church. I read the writings of such Western theologians as **Tillich, Kierkegaard**, and others. I learned the songs of the church and embraced its rituals. I even studied Greek. This whole process was my formation for the priesthood. I accepted this process willingly and acknowledged Western thought and theology as normative and absolute in my preparation for life as a priest and as a Native Christian. These were happy years, and the Christian traditions that I had embraced brought meaning and purpose to my life.

Throughout this whole formative process and earlier upbringing, I was convinced that Native traditions and spirituality were inherently evil and pagan because they were contradictory to the Christian faith. I was warned about the dangers of syncretism and told that I must not compromise my faith as a Christian. I was deeply concerned about the centrality of Christ and

---

SOREN KIERKEGAARD (1813–1855) was a Danish philosopher of religion and the father of Christian existentialism. He contrasted the demands of conventional ethics with following one's own faith, using as a model Abraham's readiness, in fear and trembling, to sacrifice Isaac in obedience to God's command. Individual decisions are made in response to revelation, not on the basis of scientific hypotheses or logical inferences. In religion, subjectivity is truth and can be communicated only indirectly. The incarnation of the eternal God in history is a paradox to non-Christians. Among Kierkegaard's writings are *Fear and Trembling, Philosophical Fragments*, and *Edifying Discourses*.

PAUL TILLICH (1886–1965) was a German theologian and religious socialist, expelled by the Nazis for his support of the Jews. He wrote his three-volume *Systematic Theology* while teaching in the United States. It is considered, with Karl Barth's *Church Dogmatics*, to be the most influential Protestant theology of the twentieth century. Tillich correlated traditional theology with contemporary cultural issues, stressing "the courage to be" (the title of one of his best-known books) in the face of anxiety over meaninglessness. He also reasserted "the Protestant principle," refusing to cede absolute authority to either church or state. As well, religious symbols cannot be invented, but owe their power to their participation in God's creative and redemptive presence (for example, water in baptism). Influenced by depth psychology, Tillich in his last years engaged in dialogue with Zen Buddhism and rejected exclusivist Christian teaching concerning salvation.

---

resolved that I would not bring dishonour to Christ by seeking other gods.

In the summer of 1975 I returned to my home community to pastor both the Anglican and United Church congregations. It was during this period that I and members of the faith community struggled with the resurgence of traditional Native Spirituality. Younger members of the reserve in their search for identity were exploring their Native heritage. These young people would travel to various pow wows in Canada and the United States and bring back to our village ways and cultural traditions that had become foreign to our people.

Years of Struggle

The years that followed were difficult years, marked by religious zeal and conflict. "Born again" members of my parish burned their Native symbols and quit making Native crafts. Christian members of the community boycotted the pow wows. Followers of the **Traditional Ways** lobbied to have Native Spirituality taught in the school. Anxious church members launched a counter campaign. A funeral exacerbated the turmoil. The deceased person, once a faithful church member, had left the church and embraced the Traditional Ways. At death the body was prepared in the Traditional Way with painted face and the use of traditional symbols and rituals. Community members were torn between their desire to support the bereaved family and their fear of Native Spirituality. I, as the parish priest, did not know what an appropriate pastoral response should be. I found myself just as confused and fearful as everyone else.

A Journey

These years of turmoil and religious conflict were the beginning of a long and painful personal journey. Early in this journey I attended a Catholic Charismatic Conference during which I enrolled in a workshop by Father John Hascall, a Native Roman Catholic priest. Not only was Father Hascall a priest, but he was also a **Pipe Carrier** and spiritual leader in the Midewin Lodge. His was one of the most disturbing and troubling addresses I had attended. Here was a man sharing his spiritual journey and, in the process, seemingly equating Native Spirituality

---

TRADITIONAL WAYS are the ceremonial, spiritual, and cultural customs of First Nations peoples prior to European contact. Members of some First Nations still observe these Aboriginal customs.

PIPE CARRIER is an Elder who has been given permission to use the Pipe in prayer and also has been given the spiritual care of a particular group of people. As such he is responsible for the spiritual well-being of the clan and keeping and caring for the Sacred Pipe.

with Christianity. His whole story evoked my worst fears of syncretism.

In that same period I attended a United Church conference for Native peoples. Two Traditional Elders led sessions on Native Spirituality. The Elders talked about the Pipe Ceremony and the **Sweetgrass Ceremony**. Provision was made for people to participate in a **Sweat Lodge**. People chose either to participate in or to observe the Sweetgrass Ceremony. Those actively participating in the ceremony formed an inner circle; those who chose to observe formed an outer circle. Each person was permitted to talk about the choices they had made. I remained in the outer circle and anxiously observed the ceremony. I deliberately chose the outer circle because I did not understand the ceremony and was afraid of compromising my Christian beliefs. There certainly was no way that I would join the group participating in the Sweat Lodge! I was too afraid, fearful of aligning myself with the Evil One.

I quickly put these experiences aside and determined to devote my energies more fully to the Christian faith. As part of this new commitment I went to confession and sought forgiveness for delving into pagan rituals. I even resolved to refrain from any involvement with Native Spirituality.

Despite this resolution to renounce any involvement in Native Spirituality, I found myself repeatedly in situations where I had to struggle further with this decision. On one particular occasion I attended a special service of the Native community in my home diocese. This service, held at the cathedral church, began with Father Hascall praying with the Pipe in the Four Directions. He began the ceremony with a brief explanation, saying that certain people would be invited to share the Pipe with him. His assistant called me to come forward to share in the Pipe.

Time stood still as I struggled with the implications of this request: Was it right for me, as a member of the national Anglican church staff, to share in this ritual? What would such an action say to people? Would I be compromising my Christian beliefs? Would it be right to refuse something that was sacred to others and offered to me as a symbol of honour and trust?

In the midst of turmoil and anxiety I placed the Pipe to my lips and drew upon the sacred substance, not knowing what would follow but trusting that somehow God was present in this

---

SWEETGRASS CEREMONY is a First Nations rite of purification. This ceremony is also known as "smudging." Smudging is similar to the use of incense in the church. It is a prayer for cleansing. Smoke, from the burning of sweetgrass — and sometimes tobacco, cedar, and sage — is wafted over an individual for the cleansing of one's mind, body, and heart.

SWEAT LODGE is a dome-shaped hut used for prayer. It is completely covered with hide or canvass. The prayer session is called a sweat. In the centre of the hut is a pit in which hot rocks, called "Grandfathers," are placed. When the sweat begins, the flap of the entrance is closed. Cold water is poured on the rocks. The Elder then begins the prayer. Participants are encouraged to voice their own prayers during the sweat.

action, and hoping that I would be protected from that which I did not know or understand. I returned to my seat and watched as the ceremony continued. I looked at the young men, just barely in their teens, who had been invited to be "helpers" to Father John. They were so engrossed in the ceremony and service; their faces reflected a deep sense of pride in their Native heritage. As I pondered the whole experience I had the sensation of One saying, *"This is you."*

After some years I attended the World Council of Churches Assembly on Justice, Peace, and the Integrity of Creation held in Korea. I was the only First Nations person from Canada in an enormous gathering of several thousand. The process was so European and overwhelming that I felt alienated and alone. In this state of loneliness, I was approached by four Native Americans, who asked me to join them in prayers the following morning. I felt so relieved to be with my own people.

The next morning as we stood in a circle, one of the men beat a drum and began to sing a prayer song. During this song another man prepared the Sacred Pipe for our prayers. Again, I wondered if I should be here. I was torn between my desperate need for support and my fear of Traditional Ways and the possibility of compromising my Christian principles. As the Pipe was handed to me, I asked for protection and prayed to the God that I knew and to Jesus my brother. During and following this ceremony I felt a certain peace of mind and heart and was assured that I had not compromised my Christian values. In the remaining days of the conference, it

was the daily prayers with the Pipe, the very thing I feared, that sustained me.

Of all the Native ceremonies I knew, the one I feared most and was determined to avoid was the Sweat Lodge. In the summer of 1992 I attended a Native gathering sponsored by the Roman Catholic Church. The program included healing circles and the Sweat Lodge. As I read the program I had the feeling that this time I would not be able to run away and that I would participate in a Sweat. Thinking about the prospect filled me with anxiety and fear.

I wrestled with myself, trying to decide whether or not to participate. I went to the teaching session on the healing circle and the Sweat Lodge and still did not know what to do. After the session, an acquaintance told me of his first experience of praying in a Sweat Lodge. His was a dramatic and wonderful experience. However, his glowing account did not allay my fears. It was only at the last moment, comforted by the knowledge that a close friend of mine would be with me, that I decided to take part in the Sweat.

The presence of my friend and the fact that the Elder leading the ceremony was one whom I trusted enabled me to go forward. Following the example of the other men I took a pinch of tobacco and offered it at the Sacred Fire as I entered the Sweat Lodge, crawling on hands and knees behind the other participants. When all had entered, the Elder ordered the flap of the lodge to be closed and the ceremony began. The intensity of the prayers matched the intensity of the heat from the steaming rocks.

After several rounds and hours of prayer the

ceremony came to a close. As we emerged from the lodge into the coolness of the night, we sat or lay upon the ground, knit together by the sacred bond of men who had shared a sacred journey. As I lay gazing up into the starlit sky, I felt a tremendous sense of restfulness and peace. It was a truly sacred time. As I reflected upon the experience, I could find nothing that was contradictory to the Christian gospel which I embraced.

Learnings

Through these and many other experiences I have gained a certain openness to faith journeys that are different from mine. I have listened to the stories of others whose ways are different, but in whose stories I have found the Christ of the Christian gospel. I have learned to put aside my fears and step out in faith; and in that step

of faith experienced the vastness of God, the Creator. I hear the sound of many voices, each with a tenor and beauty of its own, but which together sing the praises of God the Creator and Jesus the Son in one great symphony of creation. In the midst of that glorious sound is the phrase, *"This is you — both Native and Christian."* The meaning of that phrase will be a lifelong dialogue with self.

Each new experience and each year will uncover different aspects of that reality like the many facets of a precious gem. This dialogue is a dialogue that is shared by many First Nations people and that must continue in the midst of a changing world.

[A longer version of this essay was published in *Ecumenism*, published by the Canadian Centre for Ecumenism.]

Evangelicals have always been concerned both with personal salvation and with social transformation. Salvation should not be collapsed into social reform, but it must produce social reform.

Evangelicals have not always been *just* into saving souls. Their most enduring characteristic has been the dual mission of *evangelism* and *social involvement*. Two historical snapshots will substantiate this claim.

First, many Evangelicals associate their heritage not only with the Reformation, but also with the eighteenth-century **Evangelical Revival** and the Great Awakening. Those movements within the Anglican family insisted that the primary authority is the Bible and the highest allegiance is to Jesus Christ. The Evangelical Revival, led by John Wesley and **George Whitefield** and others, taught the Reformation message — salvation by faith alone in Jesus Christ. But the appropriation of that message was personal. "Saving souls" meant proclaiming that, because of sin, human beings are seriously out of fellowship with God and that God, in love, sent Jesus Christ, whose life, death, and resurrection secured their salvation. Whatever else conversion means, it is this human act of saying "yes" to the divine invitation.

This is not the whole evangelical story — salvation is personal but its effects are social. Over the next century, the Revival produced a company of evangelical activists who were leaders in nearly every area of social reform of their day: abolition of slavery, reform of industrial working conditions, educational reform, and reform of prisons and institutions for the mentally ill. Their effort extended from humanitarian aid to lobbying for reform laws. But Evangelicals maintained a clear distinction between evangelism and social mission. Salvation should not be

GEORGE WHITEFIELD (1714–1770) was one of the most eloquent followers of the Wesleys. He was famous for his preaching at open air meetings, and made several trips to the American colonies, where he established an orphanage and was one of the forces behind "The Great Awakening." Whitefield's theology was more rigidly Calvinistic than that of the Wesleys.

EVANGELICAL/EVANGELICALISM "Evangel" means "gospel," and in the widest sense all Christians are evangelical. More narrowly, the term belongs to the Protestant churches that base their teaching entirely, or almost entirely, on the Scriptures. More narrowly still, in the Anglican Communion the term "evangelical" is given to the group, beginning in the eighteenth century, that stresses personal conversion, the person of Christ, and his saving death. In the nineteenth century Evangelical Anglicans were active in social reform and are again now. In worship Evangelicals tend to emphasize preaching over liturgical elaboration.

FUNDAMENTALIST/FUNDAMENTALISM A Protestant movement beginning in the early twentieth century. It takes its name from a series of pamphlets, *Fundamentals: A Testimony to the Truth* [1910–1915], issued by a group from the faculty of Princeton Theological Seminary. The Fundamentalist movement was designed to counter theological liberalism and modernism by defending the *literal* truth of the Bible and doctrines considered foundational to the gospel.

collapsed into social reform, but it must *produce* social reform.

The second snapshot belongs to the twentieth century, and portrays what has been called "The Great Reversal." **Protestant liberalism** and the **Social Gospel** movement became a challenge to evangelical religion. Personal salvation by faith in Christ was replaced by belief in "the fatherhood of God and the brotherhood of man." Salvation shifted from personal appropriation with social effects to social salvation with individual implications.

The result was the **Fundamentalist–Modernist** controversy that raged among North American Protestants for half a century. Fear of being confused with the Modernists kept many Evangelicals from entering the social arena. But by the late 1960s and early 1970s the social voice of Evangelicals was being heard again. Statements on social responsibility were produced by various evangelical organizations (the Wheaton

Declaration, 1966, the National Evangelical Anglican Congress, Keele, U.K., 1967, the Chicago Declaration, 1973, and the International Lausanne Covenant, 1974).

Writers, social activists, and organizations also appeared: the Sojourners, Washington, D.C., World Vision, and Christians for Social Justice, an effective grassroots Canadian group. *Rich Christians in a World of Hunger* by Ron Sider was highly influential. John Stott wrote *Christian Mission in the Modern World* and *Involvement: Being a Responsible Christian in a Non-Christian Society,* in which he argued that the church is indispensable both as pointer to the Kingdom and as the *place* where Kingdom life can be experienced.

Evangelicals understand themselves to be constrained by Christ's love and his commandment to love their neighbours. But their profile is complex. Recent surveys consistently show that Evangelicals are probably more involved in

---

PROTESTANT LIBERALISM AND MODERNISM

Liberalism in general tends to be critical of any authority that seems to be arbitrary, and religious liberalism has been a strong current in Protestantism since the early nineteen century. In England and North America the movement was primarily religious, but in Germany it was also political. Liberalism aims to subject Scripture and religious doctrine to the same tests of verification as are applied to other knowledge, and tries to reconcile Christian belief with the claims of natural science. The Bampton Lectures of 1884, *The Relations between Religion and Science*, by Frederick Temple (1821–1902, Archbishop of Canterbury from 1897) is a well-known manifesto of this approach. The Modern Churchmen's Union was the organizational branch of Modernism in England. Underlying the Liberals' view is the belief that truth is one, and that true religion should not be

threatened by the claims of science. This "school" is waning somewhat today, as both Christians and scientists take on a more nuanced view of the universe.

In Anglicanism, "Protestant Liberalism" is more frequently called "Modernism," and it is by this name that a parallel movement in the Roman Catholic Church is known. Its aims were similar to that of the Protestant movement, but with added claim that experience is also an important component of theological reflection.

Modernism in Roman Catholicism was not organized to the degree that it was in the Anglican Church, because it consisted largely of correspondence among like-minded people. Friedrich von Hugel (1852–1925, an aristocratic cosmopolitan who lived in England) is often seen to have been the heart of the movement. It was suppressed as a system (which it never really was) by Rome in 1907.

personal volunteer work with the disadvantaged than are other Christian groups. They have tended, however, to resist political involvement. This may be due to the fear of being associated with "liberal" ideologies or causes. In the past two decades Evangelicals have become more politically aware, but they have often chosen different political issues than the mainline ones, or ended up on different sides of the issue.

Evangelicals are limited by the political naiveté of many, by their emphasis on personal influence rather than structural change, by attempts to address complex moral issues with biblical proof texts, and by an absolutist morality. Many have not recognized the new boundary lines between church and society. They still operate with the worldview that what is good for Christians is good for everybody, and therefore should be legislated. But, the Evangelical reluctance to identify political solutions with the Kingdom of God helps keep in perspective the depth of human sin, the limits of human effort, and trust in God's promise and power to bring to completion that which was begun in Jesus Christ.

In making or describing moral decisions, are we speaking the language of obligation, intention, or consequences? Does utilitarianism — the language of consequences — dominate our contemporary world?

CHRISTOPHER LIND

Have you ever been in an argument with some-one about an ethical issue and felt as if the two of you were speaking different languages? Maybe it's because you were. There are many moral languages being spoken, and each language speaks from a different worldview. No one would presume to say that French is right and Spanish is wrong. Rather, when you are in Mexico, Spanish is more appropriate than French if you wish to make yourself understood.

The first moral language is that of *obligation or duty*. The emphasis here is on paying back or giving what is owed. If God created the world and gave us life, these are gifts we can never repay, though we may try mightily. **John Calvin** uses this language. In this worldview God is the primary actor and we are the respondents. Our task is to fulfil our duty towards God. We also have obligations towards our neighbours, who have rights that we have an obligation to honour. The language of human rights is a variant of the moral language of obligation.

The second moral language is that of *intention*. Anyone who tries to defend herself by saying, "I didn't mean to do it," is using this language. She is speaking about the difference between her intention and the actual result. Our legal system speaks largely this language; the Criminal Code has harsher penalties for crimes that were intended than for those that were not. In this worldview, we all come from God and our aim should be to return to God. That destiny can be fulfilled if our end is viewed with clarity and our aim is sure.

The third moral language is simultaneously the most powerful and the most problematic. This is the language of *consequences* that is dominant in Western culture. People who judge the morality of an action primarily by its results are speaking this language. It is the language of the marketplace. If someone sells his house and someone else buys it, it doesn't matter what their intentions are. If they agree on a price and the price is paid and received, it is judged a moral

---

JOHN CALVIN (1509–1564) was a lawyer and theologian who, in 1533/34 left the Roman Catholic Church to join the Reformation movement. He was French by birth and education, but spent the most influential years of his life in Geneva, Switzerland, where he instituted a theocracy, a society in which the church dominates the state. Calvin is recognized as the founder of the non-Lutheran Protestant churches (for example, the Presbyterian and Huguenot), although there were later, more radical, reformed churches established as well (the Anabaptists). Calvin's theology was firmly in the Augustinian tradition, teaching particularly the denial of human ability to choose good after the fall and the affirmation of double predestination (following from divine omnipotence and human inability to will the good). This doctrine teaches that not only does God predetermine some to be saved, but some to be damned as well. Not all present-day Calvinists accept this doctrine. Calvin's chief writing was *The Institutes of the Christian Religion*, published in several editions in French and Latin.

act. This language is an ancient one, and in the nineteenth century it acquired the name of "utilitarianism."

As churches become minorities in Western societies they are forced to speak the language of the majority. When the Canadian churches try to persuade the government not to bankrupt them with lawsuits over residential schools, the churches use the argument of consequences: such a strategy will be harmful to society and the government. The churches may believe that the government has an obligation to protect the churches from harm (language number one), or they may believe that Canadian society cannot become what it was meant to be by this strategy (language number two). However, the language that is most likely to be heard and understood is the language of consequences and utility (language number three). This language is problematic for Christians because it is the most recent and unfamiliar. It isn't prominent in the Scriptures or in church traditional teachings, and it remains a minor language in the documents of the Reformation. It is, however, the language of commerce, and it dominates today's world.

REFLECTION

Joanne Chris, how does the third language differ from "the end justifies the means"?

Christopher Joanne, your question illustrates the difference between an ethic of duty and an ethic oriented to outcomes. For example, if you think it wrong to torture someone, that action will be morally wrong regardless of whatever seeming benefits it may produce. That is the ethic of duty. Someone whose ethic is oriented to outcomes might argue that the benefits arising will outweigh the harm produced. That argument is used to justify the bombing, accidental or intentional, of innocent civilians in wars.

Walter Chris, I find your presentation helpful but problematic. As a biblical scholar, I find all three languages present and interwoven in the Old and New Testaments. I think that all three are also constantly interwoven in most people's experience of moral decision making. I also am uncomfortable when you make the language of consequences and utilitarianism equivalent. The moral language of consequences is found in most of the Israelite prophets and wisdom writers, but it's not necessarily utilitarian. All three languages are used, and one often provides a critique of the other. Even the language of the market appears when moral questions are often framed in terms of money or valuable objects.

Christopher Let me explain further what I mean by the language of consequence and utility. The language of consequences is an ancient language present in Scripture and in the writings of the earliest Greek philosophers. The language of utility is a modern variant. In the nineteenth century

John Stuart Mill argued that you could determine the positive moral consequences of an action by calculating its utility. It is this language that now dominates moral discourse in our world. That is why you can find obvious examples of the language of consequences in the Old Testament but not utilitarian language.

Walter I think there is another totally distinct language: the language of limit. In Judaism the capacity to limit oneself is seen as a way that makes us more human and enlarges our moral capacity. The point is not that self-deprivation is good in itself, but that self-limitation manifests freedom. For example, much ink has been vainly spilled in trying to present the dietary laws in utilitarian or intentional terms. Equally, such laws are not readily explained in the language of obligation. Christ's self-emptying is the most dramatic instance of this. I would suggest that when we choose to limit ourselves, we manifest most fully the divine image.

Christopher The capacity and need for self-limiting behaviour is not so obviously a language as much as a virtue which would place it within the teleological discourse as I have described it in the overview.

Authentic spirituality means recognizing the interrelatedness of all things in creation. Right living means acting to ensure that no part of creation is violated, that all are honoured.

LAVERNE JACOBS

The Walpole Island First Nation community is situated downstream from major chemical plants along the St. Clair River. One plant in particular is cause for much concern. ICI Canada Inc. applied to the Ontario Ministry of Environment and Energy for approval to discharge its pondwater into the St. Clair River. On 27 September 1996 permission was granted for ICI to discharge 750 million gallons of treated phosphate process water into the river. First Nations people fear this discharge will result in toxic substances accumulating in river sediments, and will find their way into the plants and animals upon which First Nations people rely for their food and economy.

However, of greater concern is the spiritual impact of such action on First Nations people. Water and all aspects of creation are such an integral part of First Nations being that, when creation suffers, First Nations people suffer.

As John Lame Deer, one of the Lakota Elders, states in *Meditations with Native Americans — Lakota Spirituality* :

We Indians live in a world of symbols and
   images
where the spiritual and the commonplace
   are one.
To the white man symbols are just words,
spoken or written in a book.
To us they are a part of nature,
part of ourselves —
the earth, the sun, the wind, and the rain,
stones, trees, animals, even little insects
like ants and grasshoppers.
We try to understand them

not with the head
but with the heart,
and we need no more than a hint
to give us the meaning.

The women of Walpole Island spoke about this relationship in their presentation to the International Joint Commission looking into this issue. Their position is one which touches me deeply and one with which I can relate. It is from this context that I relate to and work with the Primate's Theological Commission. The following is the Native Women's position paper (edited for length), which I have permission to share with the Commission.

MINOBIMAATISIIWIN—
We are to care for her
BKJEWANONG—
Where the waters divide

We are the mothers and grandmothers, daughters and granddaughters, the aunties and the nieces of our community. Many of our Elder Women recall when the water was still pure, when they spent their days swimming in the river and were able to drink from it without worrying about contaminants. They remember when the river froze solidly every winter, twenty-four inches of ice as clear as glass. We speak for the children and grandchildren of today, and for those yet unborn.

When the International Joint Commission was formed, the First Nations along the Great Lakes were formally consulted for the very first time with regard to the conditions and concerns about the water. It has always been part of our culture to wait until we are asked before we present our views. Now that we have been asked, it is our duty to speak out on behalf of our Earth Mother and the water so crucial to all life. We speak today not as victims, but as authors of our own future. We speak on behalf of our brothers and sisters, the plants and animals whose care and concern has long been ignored by the world. We speak of our concerns for the plants and wildlife that are disappearing from our watershed because these are necessities for food, clothing, medicine, crafts with which we teach, and the list goes on....

Among all Native cultures, no force is considered more sacred or more powerful than the ability to create new life. All females are the human manifestation of the Earth Mother, who is the first and ultimate giver of life. In our instructions we are told, "Minobimaatisiiwin — we are to care for her." Indigenous people, worldwide, have teachings instructing us in our stewardship of the Earth, and these teachings tell us that the Creator has provided a balance between male and female, each with our own role. We are here to carry out our roles as Women and Native people. We have been honoured with these two responsibilities, both of which we take very seriously.

In the past Native Leaders were chosen by the women in their communities, partly because the women have an intimate spiritual connection with the children from the time of pre-conception and would do only what was in their best interest. Also because women were held in very high regard for their life-giving responsibilities and phenomenal spiritual power.

Women do not select war as an alternative because war brings with it the loss of children. Instead we choose to have you understand our position and responsibility. We understand that the Creator Grandfather made all that there is and breathed life into it. He made the land and the water to be pure. When our Father the Sun sends his power to join with the seed of the Earth Mother, new life is born. Our teachings also tell us that the Earth Mother has structure just as we do. The rocks are her bones, the waters are her blood, the streams and groundwater that flow throughout her body are her veins taking nourishment to all her living parts.

This sacred "Water" that is being so heartlessly abused still continues to give life to all people because this is the way the Creator would have it. Our beliefs, our practices, our usage, our customs, and our culture have proven this to be so. When we pray, we finish with the closing "Kina Enwemgig — all my relations." This refers not only to our human relations, but also to the creatures that swim, crawl, and fly, the plants and trees, the mountains, lakes, and streams, the moon, stars, and planets of the universe — simply put, everything. Everything is relational and can be understood only in this way. These understandings are the basis for our spirituality, which honours the Natural Law necessary for balance.

In our teachings, Original Man walked the Earth, giving names to all the creatures, plants, and insects. He was given a companion, the Wolf. When they separated, they were told, "What shall happen to one of you will also happen to the other." Since then both the Anishnaabek (i.e., the human being) and the Wolf have come to be alike and experience the same things. Both of them mate for life; both have a clan system and a tribe. Both have had their land taken from them. Both have been hunted for their hair. And both have been pushed close to extinction by chemical genocide. A world terribly out of balance, wouldn't you say?

In many world religions, when people are baptized with holy water, they are welcomed into the faith. Our teachings say these waters must be kept absolutely pure because these river waters are our holy water. By taking even the minutest chance of contaminating it, you are desecrating all that is sacred to us. We use the sacred water in our purification lodge, in ceremonies of healing, in rites of passage, in naming ceremonies, and especially in women's ceremonies. At these times, the teachings are spoken to the water and then it is passed around from one to another in the circle to be shared. At the change of the seasons, a pilgrimage to the water is carried out in order to honour the Spirit of the Water. Our people have always understood that this sacred and powerful water gives life and can take it away.

When industrial society makes decisions about water quality, do they consider that our bodies are made up mostly of water? The Creator has bestowed many gifts on us, including this sacred water. Therefore we must honour the teaching that says if the gifts are misused, as tobacco is, these gifts will turn on us and make us sick. There are proven links between pollutants and diseases of the reproductive systems, specific types of cancer, and other systemic diseases.

Our Elders tell us that if the Women become sick, then the Children will be sick, and Nations will cease to exist. Is this what we really want?

By presenting this paper we are submitting the following:

+ We are demanding spiritual and moral accountability from the industrial world that so blatantly ignores the condition of the Earth, the sacred water, and our people.

+ We are asking for the understanding by all women, by all cultures, of the concerns we raise about the care of our Earth Mother and about the sacred water.

+ We are asking that women from all cultures stand beside us as we continue to protect our Earth Mother in her battle to survive, and also for your vigilance for resources that will help this cause.

- We are asking for prayers of support from women of all faiths so that these issues may come to peaceful resolution.

- We reach out to connect with women throughout this region, this country, and this world. We need the strength of all women — to analyze, to empathize, to voice their values, to state opinions, to summarize findings, and to speak from the heart.

- We ask these things in a spirit of strength, humility and respect for our Elders' position of *zero discharge*.

The following poem was published by an environmental organization representing eleven Ojibwa Bands. It eloquently illustrates what is in our hearts.

NIBI

Anishinaabekwe, the Daughters,
You are the keepers of the water.
I am Nibi ... water ... the sacred source,
the blood of Aki, Mother Earth,
the force, filling dry seeds to green
    bursting.
I am the womb's cradle.
I purify.
Nibi, the lifegiver ...
forever the Circle's charge.
I have coursed through our Mother's veins.
Now hear my sorrow and my pain
in the rivers' rush, the rain ...

I am your grandchildren's drink.
Listen, Daughters, always,
you are keepers of the water.
Hear my cry,
for the springs flow darkly now
through the heart of Aki ...
Miigwetch / We thank you.

Laverne Jacobs continues:

The view of creation and stewardship expressed in the presentation of the women seems to be in contradiction with the first chapter of Genesis.

And God said, "let us make man in our image, in our likeness, and let them *rule over* the fish of the sea and the birds of the air, over the livestock, over all the earth, and over all the creatures that move along the ground....

God blessed them and said to them, "Be fruitful and increase in number; fill the earth and *subdue* it. *Rule over* the fish of the sea and the birds of the air and over every living creature that moves on the ground" (*italics added*) [Genesis 1:26, 28].

Does this translation represent a particular cultural bias? To me as a Native person, the notion of humankind dominating and controlling creation is most disturbing. There we find all creation living in harmony and all equally dependent .

THE CIRCLE WILL BE COMPLETE

There is a dream of the time
when the world will stretch forth its hand
to seek the Spirit of the Indian Nation.

It is in anticipation of this time
that we will prepare our gifts.
We will show all who would learn,
the language of the soul,
the rightness of nature,
in which nothing is out of place.

They will learn of a dimension of existence
which has long been lost,
where the very dust under our feet
is conscious of the sympathetic touch
of our footsteps,
for the soil is rich
with the lives of our kindred.
When the time comes,
our brothers will seek to know the strength
of our People,
our hearts will once again dance
with the pride of long ago.

Because the Great Sprit would have it,
we will give freely,
as we did in past times.

In beauty,
the circle will be complete.

Marj Williams

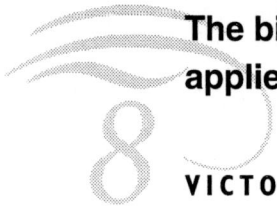

The biblical idea of Jubilee can and should be applied in today's world.

8 VICTORIA MATTHEWS

Some time ago I searched for the word "Jubilee" in a series of rather dated theological word books. It was absent. Passing from joy to Jerusalem, the word and concept of Jubilee was evidently not considered noteworthy.

Things have changed. With the approach of the year 2000 and the third Christian millennium, the Christian churches seized upon the theological concept and practice of Jubilee as found in Leviticus. The teaching is clearly Sabbath based. After six years of working the land, the seventh is a Sabbath. After seven times seven years, the fiftieth is declared a Jubilee and

> [Y]ou shall return, every one of you, to your property and every one of you to your family. The fiftieth year shall be a jubilee year for you; you shall not sow or reap the aftergrowth, or harvest the unpruned vines. For it is a jubilee, it shall be holy to you. [Leviticus 25:10b-12a.]

Not only is the land allowed to return to its natural state, but those who have been forced to sell themselves into slavery are redeemed in the Jubilee year. Some scholars think that Jesus was proclaiming Jubilee when he read from Isaiah in the synagogue in Nazareth and announced, "Today this scripture has been fulfilled in your hearing" [Luke 4:21].

While it is believed that Jubilee was never fully enacted in the centuries prior to Christ, the concept of setting captives free and restoring the goodness of creation is a major biblical theme. Thus when it was adopted by the churches in the lead-up to the year 2000, and in particular when it was yoked with the vision of the cancellation of debt for the world's poorest countries, is it no wonder the idea gathered momentum. Indeed it was clearly one time when the church's prophetic voice was heard by the world. In Canada, subsequent years saw the Jubilee initiative focus upon child poverty and land rights.

At the time of writing it is early 2002. Poverty in Canada worsens as the gap between the wealthy and the impoverished grows. Land claims and the notion of people in bondage desiring to be set free is writ large on the agenda of church and society No one could claim that the attempt at declaring a Jubilee was an unqualified success. Only a portion of the crippling debt that burdens countries such as Tanzania was cancelled. In many countries the amount of aid given to a needy country is dwarfed by the amount of interest that must be paid on the national debt. In an attempt to pay at least the interest on the debt, the environment is ravaged and health care and schooling, even at the most basic levels, is reduced or cancelled. The gospel question, "Who is my neighbour?" confronts the First World countries that call in loans.

Elsewhere in this resource the Primate's Theological Commission invites readers to consider the theology of money. The concept of Jubilee also does that, but it goes further. It challenges us to consider the just use of power; it reminds us that the land is not really ours, but belongs to God, and it leaves us with the profound question of what has given us the presumption to ignore the commandment about the Sabbath and the whole concept of a holy rest.

Present and future theological workbooks will not be so quick to ignore Jubilee. But will it be remembered as a passing attempt at social justice or as the call to Jews and Christians to remember who we are and to whom we belong?

Contextual Theology

9

CHRISTOPHER LIND

Contextual Theology is so-called because it tries to respond to questions and problems that currently confront the church and the world, contrasted with theology that focuses on the traditional questions, for example, the Trinity. (Yet, in the fourth and fifth centuries the theology of the Trinity was highly contextual.) Even today the two styles of theology sometimes overlap; a great deal of Trinitarian theology attempts to provide a divine model for human community.

Contextual theology (which has existed under different names for centuries) tends to start from and address itself to problems of suffering. Certain questions involving suffering face the Anglican Church in Canada today in a very particular way. The Commission has chosen to present three of those questions here: Christian stewardship, the aftermath of the residential schools, and the farming crisis in Saskatchewan — how do and how should Christians direct their money?

FINANCIAL STEWARDSHIP

This page is intended as a discussion starter (for your own internal dialogue, or for a group). Members of the Commission brainstormed some common phrases we hear used about money and the economy. Which do you identify with? Which do you disagree with? What are the assumptions about money that lie behind them? What are the assumptions about the purpose and end of human life that lie behind them?

REFLECTION

✦ For Christians, does God have anything to do with money, and if so, what?

Better to give than to receive.

Why tithe if you pay taxes?

Give as you can [Article XXXVIII].

I paid my way: you pay yours.

The bottom line.

$$ \$\$\$? $$

You can't take it with you.

Is the church marketable?

Is money something to pray about?

When you give a feast, invite the poor [Luke 14:13].

Shopping is good.

BREAKING THE LAW OF LOVE
Laverne Jacobs and Eileen Scully

Laverne I would like to rephrase the first two verses of the Gospel of John to read:

> In the beginning was Love and Love was with God. And Love was God. Love was with God in the beginning. Through Love all things were made; without Love nothing was made that has been made.

The starting place for me is Love. This Love first exists in community — the community of God the Father, God the Son, and God the Holy Spirit. Love cannot exist outside of community. Love finds its fullest expression and fulfillment in relationship.

In the Genesis creation stories the whole created order lives in loving relationship. Humankind is portrayed as a couple living in harmony with the animal kingdom and walking in the cool of the evening with God. However, the relationship is broken. What follows in biblical history and in all history are God's efforts to restore the relationship and bring about reconciliation. God tries to reconcile his people through a series of covenant relationships, beginning with Noah: "I will establish my covenant as an everlasting covenant between me and you and your descendants after you for the generations to come, to be your God and the God of your descendants after you" [see Genesis 17:7].

Over and over again, God reaffirms this commitment to be in relationship with his people: "So you will be my people, and I will be your God"

[Jeremiah 30:22]. God, moreover, makes a commitment to love: "I have loved you with an everlasting love. I will always love you" [Jeremiah 31:33].

All history is a story of relationships: between husband and wife, between parent and child, between individuals and communities, between tribes and nations. It is the story of people's desire to be in relationship and people's propensity to break relationships.

When the Newcomers came to Canada, they formed alliances with the nations they encountered. The Six Nations welcomed them and entered into an agreement with them marked by a "Friendship Chain."

As tradition puts it, these nations attached the ship of the British to a strong tree with a silver Covenant Chain of Friendship, so that if some storm should arise, the strong chain of friendship would keep the ship from being set adrift in rough waters. The British and the Six Nations met from time to time to polish the chain, to remove from it any tarnish or dirt, which might cause it to weaken. In other words, the overriding friendship was to be so strong that it could survive temporary storms. That tradition meant our ancestors, yours and mine, decided, centuries ago, that they would meet from time to time to deal with any problems that might have arisen between them. They decided that, together, they would resolve problems, polish the chain, so to speak, so that their great friendship would endure for all time. That chain of friendship kept the British ship attached to North America more than once. When the Crown was threatened, we were there to defend it.

The British made promises and entered into treaties with the First Nations, but the promises and treaties were not kept and the chain became tarnished. First Nations felt hurt and betrayed. Today, First Nations people are taking the churches to court for damages incurred in the residential schools; more tarnish is being added to the chain. Now, non-Native Canadians are feeling hurt and betrayed. "How could they," they ask, "after all we've done for them?"

The chain has become weakened. The relationship between Newcomer Canadians and the First Nations has been damaged. This brokenness in relationship is sin.

Eileen I agree. The biblical notion of covenant and the friendship chain both speak of the need to tend to the relationship. Sin is failing to honour our relationships with God and with each other. Sin is brokenness and fragmentation.

Often in modern life sin takes the form of analysis and linear thinking. Even in theology we are apt to get so caught up in analysis of particular questions, such as the meaning of sin, for example, that we break down Christian faith and living into component parts. The result is fragmentation, not understanding. The problems with fragmentation and linear thinking are that we tend to lose sight of the big picture of God's love, of which God continually reminds us. By contrast, Christian faith and life are a mystery. It's a whole so great that its meaning can never be exhausted. Sin is turning away from the wholeness of the mystery towards mere fragments of understanding.

Laverne You have spoken of God reminding us of God's love for us. That's not the message that the missionaries brought to First Nations people in Canada. The message was almost the reverse of that. They were told not that God loved them, but that they had to change and become like the Europeans. Their ways weren't good enough; their ways were evil, and they had to change.

That's where at least some aspect of sin enters in. Covenants between people, unlike covenants between God and people, have to begin with relationships that are in some ways equal. The people who see themselves as superior cannot recognize that they could receive gifts from the other culture, or even that the other culture has gifts to give. Superiority blinds them to the gifts that others have.

In the early contacts between First Nations people and Europeans, First Nations people were on the other side, saying, "Look at these poor newcomer. How can we help them to survive in a country that they don't know anything about." There were two very different starting points to the relationships and two different perceptions about what was happening. One was saying, "What can we get?" The other was saying, "What can we give?"

The First Nations people believed that we're all related, whether from across the ocean or not. Sharing shaped their view of relationship. The Newcomers, lacking that sense of relationship, believed they were superior, and so they thought it was morally right to conquer and impose their views on the people they conquered.

Look at the two different ways of viewing the treaties. The Newcomers thought, "We've agreed that this will be yours and this will be mine." There was always a sense of ownership. First Nations people thought, "We will share this, respect it, and use it properly." They weren't giving anything up — the land wasn't theirs to give up; it belonged to everybody. In the dialogue between the chiefs and the missionaries on my reserve, Walpole Island, the chiefs recognized the positive value of the message that the missionaries were bringing. But they were saying also, "We have our ways, and they are good for us and healthy. This is right for us."

Eileen The church now wants to make things right, but even when well-meaning people want to do the right thing, they still want to be the ones who do the giving and decide what's good for whom. That's part of the present chapter of the residential schools story. Their hidden agenda is the belief, "We know what's best for these people." Genuine relationship requires the humility that recognizes the mystery and dignity of the other person. That person is created in the image and likeness of God — and that is an awesome mystery. If we can't allow that, then we run the risk of not respecting the dignity of that person. A relationship without mutual respect of dignity is a one-sided relationship of arrogance.

When most people hear the word "person," they think "individual." An individual is a person cut off from relationship. When you say "person," Laverne, you mean the person in community. But Western culture is so scarred by competitive rat-race individualism that it's hard to build genuine community, even though most people really want it. Competitive individualism is part of the brokenness of society — part of its sin. It eats into the life of the church in ways that we don't even recognize easily, and it makes building relationships with First Nations people very difficult.

Laverne Yes, the sense of the sacredness of all of life has been lost. When you look at the trouble between First Nations and the rest of society, it generally is around something considered sacred. At Oka, it was about sacred land. At Burnt Church, it's around the right use of the sea and its fruits.

Eileen The dominant culture frames the problem in terms of legal or human rights issues, not recognizing the interconnectedness of land, water, and community. It thinks of environmental protection instead of environmental connection. Relationships are not only with other people but with the wider community of earth, human and non-human, and with God. All are part of the mystery.

Laverne Science and technology, which could shed light on all this, are too narrowly focused.

Eileen And in a society of competitive individualism, they are used for private gain. For example, you can look at the human genome and be in awe of the amazing diversity of creation and of the amount of genetic material we all share. Or you can look at it with dollar signs in your eyes.

It's as if fear intrudes as we contemplate nature's richness — fear of death, fear of not having enough, fear of change, fear of otherness. The response is to try to grab and control.

Laverne What do you think was the fear that initiated the response that resulted in the residential schools?

Eileen There was a basic fear of otherness, resulting in cultural arrogance. Beneath that, however, lies the fear that maybe we aren't the best — the fear that, if we let another people be who they are, perhaps we won't be the best. Competitiveness is the culprit. It's the root sin that creates the "structure" of sin in which even good intentions can become warped unwillingly.

In the residential schools some individuals abused children. But those acts of abuse took place within a wider context of sin institutionalized in structures — the official policies of assimilation — that resulted from the fragmented thinking that causes competitiveness and colonial arrogance. The legacies of these "structural" realities of sin live among us today as vividly as the legacies of sexual, physical, cultural, and emotional abuse.

The challenge for the present-day church and society is to deal with the whole legacy of the residential schools — not just the abuse of children by individuals, but also the fear-filled competitiveness and arrogance that characterized the relationship between Newcomers and Native peoples. In his 1993 apology, the Primate said: "I am in need of healing, the church is in need of healing." Are members of the dominant society ready to accept that?

Most Christians begin to think about sin in terms of individual acts of transgression. But if we start where you are, with love and covenant, sin is brokenness that perpetuates itself. The pain and suffering of those who have been sinned against can lead to their perpetrating more pain and suffering. Recognizing that all of us are marked by sin opens the door to healing through the redemptive power of God in Christ. In healing and redemption we are reconciled with God, with one another, with the earth. Christ's body was broken as a result of our brokenness. By Christ's resurrection, the way is opened for us to experience resurrection.

Confronting the sins of our past and confronting the way they are perpetuated in the present requires telling the truth about our brokenness, our sin. Can we welcome truth-telling as the gift of God? Can we be open and vulnerable to receiving this gift? And to receiving the gift of truth and reconciliation from others? If we can, covenant and relationship can be restored, and sin can be taken away.

REFLECTION

Joanne McWilliam Eileen and Laverne, the theme of your discussion is that Native culture is superior to Western. Is this consistent with Laverne's statement that "covenants between people ... have to begin with relationships that are more or less equal." I think we must be careful not to demonize Western or Native, or indeed any other, culture.

THE SASKATCHEWAN FARM CRISIS

Christopher Lind

I live and work in Saskatchewan, a primarily agriculture province. More than half of Canada's wheat comes from here. The farmers have been hammered and hammered by the way the market is organized, so the wealth of Saskatchewan has been progressively destroyed. Saskatchewan farmers make a return on their investment of less than one per cent. The prices of agriculture products go up but the profit returned stays flat or declines. The crisis is very real.

For these communities there is a profound question of meaning. What does God intend in these times as families, trying to be faithful disciples, faithful gardeners in Eden, are torn apart? They see the profits of agricultural corporations go through the roof. Where is God in all this?

Some farmers are wondering about the future of all creation with the turn to genetically modified organisms. There is nothing in the Thirty-Nine Articles that provides an obvious answer.

Contextual theology demands an analysis of the situation from which these questions and problems stem. What is actually going on in the farm community? In family and community relationships? What is going on politically and socially? After analysis people turn to scripture and ask, "When have people of faith asked these questions before and what have they discerned? When has the church faced these problems before and what has it learned?"

They find some answers. One of the factors of the farm crisis is the enormous expense for young farmers to start in farming. They have to borrow enormous sums of money and pay usurious interest on mortgages that they cannot afford, given their profit margin. Their high hopes are slowly eroded; they are defeated and declare bankruptcy. One of the responses of the ACC has been to join with other churches in Saskatchewan to support an organization called "Earth Care Connection," which sponsors the Genesis Land Conservancy. It assembles farmland on the basis of a land trust: young farmers sign a lease for the land, and work with the community to decide how to take care of the land in a sustainable fashion. They are not required to make mortgage payments, but pay rent instead. They have a future in farming for the rest of their lives.

The Genesis Land Conservancy's response is a practical response that has emerged out of contextual theological reflection. It is an Anglican response, but it is ecumenical as well, and it serves all the communities of Saskatchewan.

Jesus' healing ministry has been continued by the church. Although the modern West is sceptical of the power of spiritual healing, recent developments reflect a shift in attitude.

DAVID REED

Few dispute that healing and exorcism were central to the ministry of Jesus. But modern questions abound. Was Jesus a skilled proto-psychologist who understood and released the psychosomatic potential in people? Were the healings extraordinary "advertisements" for his ministry and that of the Apostles, no longer needed as the church became established?

These questions and their underlying assumptions are heard frequently but miss the central point of Jesus' ministry: Jesus does not just speak on behalf of God; he reveals and embodies the very nature and character of God. This carries three important implications.

First, Jesus' healing ministry demonstrates God's *compassion* for the pain and suffering of the world. If one questions whether or not God is a loving God, we need only look at Jesus' healing ministry.

Second, Jesus' healings are a *sign* of that future world when all suffering, pain, and disorder will be banished forever. Not all are healed, and all eventually die. But there is a contingency, an open-endedness, in all healings (including the raising of the dead) that calls us to look forward to God's future reign. We do not grasp the full significance of a healing or even a healing prayer that yields no physical result, apart from the promise of wholeness embedded in the healing act.

Third, to experience healing in the present, even in small measure, is to be offered a *foretaste* of future wholeness. We experience the "already" of the "not yet," the first installment of the Holy Spirit as the promise of a full inheritance. God

will transform even these small bounded miracles into that "world without end."

But did Jesus intend to continue his healing ministry through the ministry of the church? And if so, what form should it take? Some interpretations have explained Jesus' mighty works in terms of his deity. In that case, his healings were unique and limited to him. But others claim that these works were the effect of the Spirit's empowering presence in his life, a power promised and given to the church at Pentecost.

We have some clues that the latter conviction is closer to the truth. One is that the healing ministry has never been entirely absent from the church's life, though sometimes without its hearty acceptance. Also, unlike practitioners of some other religions, Christians have steadfastly refused to accept sickness and disease as the result of fate or divine will. Signs can be seen in the founding of hospitals, orphanages, and various other Christian humanitarian ministries.

The degree of acceptance of the healing ministry is influenced by a number of factors. One is the receptivity of the host culture. For example, the eighteenth-century Enlightenment with its scientistic worldview of a closed universe argued that healing is impossible since such a divine act would imply breaking the laws of nature, laws that God alone established. A second factor is the tradition, called *cessationism*, which states that it was God's plan to phase out miracles and healings once the church was established and mature.

In the scientistic West, healing has not been rejected but reinterpreted in terms of medical treatment. In regions where scientific medicine is less available, spiritual healing is more readily received and usually more effective. Sometimes healing occurs where medicine fails. Healing of illnesses may be complete or partial, may accelerate a healing in progress, or may touch another region of the personality. Recent scientific theories of an "open" universe have created a more receptive climate for healing in our own culture.

Christian healing practices vary from episcopally authorized anointing with oil and laying on of hands to various expressions of intercesssory prayer ministry. Both are practiced in the Anglican tradition. Anointing or "unction" in the *BCP* [230] is the rite of administering oil (usually olive oil) by a priest or authorized "lay anointer." The oil is a symbol of healing presence, and the anointer represents the presence and ministry of the whole church.

Expectations stretch from acquiescing to the mystery of divine sovereignty to acquiring the faith of a mustard seed. Whatever form it takes, in the centre or on the margins of the church, Jesus' healing ministry continues.

Christians hold a wide variety of views on mission and the relationship between Christianity and other faiths.

Commission members identified a passage from Scripture that reflects their perspective on mission, read the passage aloud, and spoke briefly about it. The following identifies the passages, and provides their statements and an edited version of the conversation that followed.

Walter [Genesis 12:1–3]

One has to go back to the prior mission within which Jesus is understood. This Genesis passage is one expression of that. The mission is about drawing the whole earth into a relationship with God, a relationship of security in a promised place and within a community. For me, mission is about bringing people into a relationship with God so that they can be blessed. It involves putting mission in a larger frame in which the whole earth is filled with mutual relationships of blessing.

David [Acts 1: 3–9]

This is the resurrected Jesus giving a mandate to his apostles. He had spent time with them talking about the Kingdom of God, to advance which was his ministry. It's a Trinitarian mandate. The Apostles will wait until they receive the Holy Spirit, the gift of the Father. Thus, there is a line of mission — from God the Father to Christ, then through the Spirit to us. Mission will be God's work, not ours. And note the extension — from Jerusalem to Samaria to the ends of the earth. The mandate is universal; it is not a mere extension of Western culture.

Eileen [2 Corinthians 5:16–20]

This passage says very strongly to me that we are sent as ambassadors and given a ministry of reconciliation. The work is God's work and arises from what God has first done for us. So we are humble ambassadors, seeing others not from the point of view of our self-interest or the self-interest of the church. The church needs to discern the essential ministry of reconciliation of ourselves with each other and with God and with the whole world. This ministry must not be skewed by our cultural presuppositions.

Robert [John 4: 23–24]

This passage should be seen within the whole context of Jesus' encounter with the Samaritan woman. It emphasizes the universal and Trinitarian aspect of mission. What is the ultimate purpose of mission? It is not about the aggrandizement of the church (although it is important that the church grow), nor for the spread of Christian culture (though that should happen), nor for social justice (although this is important too.) The ultimate aim of mission, as of all existence, is worship. Mission is not for world-improvement, though that is part along the way; it is for the glory of God.

Laverne [Matthew 25: 31–40]

I probably chose this passage in reaction to the experience of mission by the colonizers. The verse I was drawn to was the last one: whatever you did for the least of these brothers of mine, you did it for me. There is a sense that when the missionaries came to Canada they didn't bring Christ. Christ was already here, and there was a failure to recognize that. Mission is recognizing and honouring the Christ who is already there, and I bring honour to Christ by the way I honour, treat, and interact with those with whom I come into contact. There are all kinds of hunger and all kinds of thirst. There can be spiritual hunger, so it may be a matter of pointing out to people the grace they already have, and saying, "This is Christ," and allowing that to shape and nourish the reconciliation that God desires.

Victoria [John 17:18]

This passage contains the whole apostolic notion of being sent to the world, not simply to the church. It is very much a mission of being in the world — incarnation — not just acting. We are sent to comfort the afflicted and to afflict the comfortable, as much by who we are as by what we do. It is ultimately a matter of transformation, our own and that of others with whom we come into contact. In this way we are all brought to know the glory of God in the face of Jesus Christ.

Joanne [Acts 1:8]

For us to carry out a mission, to be witnesses to God in Christ, we need the gift of the Holy Spirit. Witness and martyr are the same word in Greek, and while some Christians are called to martyrdom, we are all called to witness in the contemporary sense. In doing so, we are making ourselves part of a tradition; as Christ witnessed to the coming Kingdom of God, so we bring our witness of that Kingdom to the world by how we live and by what we teach. We are witnessing as well to what Christ is — the human face of God. Our witness begins at home (Jerusalem), extends to our neighbours (Samaria), and ultimately expands to the whole world.

DIALOGUE

Joanne I get annoyed with people who rightly agonize over the sufferings in Africa and the Middle East, but not over the suffering under our noses, such as that of the homeless in Canadian cities.

David I think that attitude is a carry-over from Christendom, when we took care of the local area pastorally, but thought of our "mission" as somewhere else.

Laverne But with what kind of attitude will we approach people in the street? Can we look into the eyes of a prostitute and see Christ?

Eileen And can we recognize that street people have gifts for us?

Victoria Mother Teresa talked about the sisters spending time each morning before the Sacrament so that they could recognize the face of Christ in the streets. However, the question with which I honestly struggle is a little different: What is it that we are offering beyond love?

Laverne When I think of traditional Native people, or people of other faiths, I am reminded of John's passage, "I am the way, the truth, and the life." If Jesus is ultimate truth and these people are trying to be faithful as they understand it, then I see Christ there.

Robert There is also the question of what mission is meant to accomplish. Is it to improve the lot of mankind?

Joanne That's certainly part of it.

Robert But the lot of mankind is ultimately improved only in salvation.

Walter Robert's observation rings true to Genesis, but the prophetic works always link the knowledge of God with justice and mercy. Is it only through the seed of Abraham that the world is blessed? Has Abraham's blessing really become a blessing for everyone else?

Joanne Didn't Paul turn his back on Abraham's exclusivity when he went to the Gentiles?

Robert Yes and no. That is all preparation. It has been superseded and the mission has become universal. I think there is a place for Christian inclusivism, but only one that does not deny the particularity of the mission of Christ and the church. The question is, How much does knowledge of God depend on Jesus Christ? Is Christ only one way among others?

Joanne In another paper (which will be in book four) you yourself have offered an answer to that question. There are many ways to God, but there is a certain particularity in Jesus as the way.

Victoria You know my love for Santiago de Compostela. When I was there, it disturbed me that most of the lit candles were set at the shrine of St. James the Moorslayer. Depicted there are the heads of the Muslim enemy crushed underfoot. But the people whose heads are shown there were also created in the image and likeness of God. That shrine does not reflect the conversation we are having here. And we still live in a world where Christians practise violence against one another. Should we not be outraged?

Robert Shouldn't one use force against oppression? The Galicians may have been particularly grateful to God for deliverance from a horrible oppression. Situations are ambiguous. Do we renounce violence totally?

WAYS TO USE THIS BOOK

Working alone, you might read this book from beginning to end to get an overview of the issues or to follow a theme that runs through it. Or you might choose to begin at a place that interests you and continue reading in any order that suggests itself.

Two people could work together with the book. Beginning with one of the statements, you might read it aloud, then consider the questions it raises for you. With what points would you agree or disagree? The Reflection following each statement might suggest lines for further thinking. You might like to tackle the "writing your own statement" exercise explained below.

Working alone or with a group, you will probably find that you are raising your own questions on the topic. You can compare them with the questions defined by the members of the Primate's Theological Commission and see the responses proposed by members of the Commission. Naturally, you will bring your own experience to your consideration of the questions, and tell your own stories.

In other words, you will be doing theology and thinking deeply about your own Christian faith and life.

WORKING WITH THIS BOOK IN A GROUP

Groups require time at every gathering to build or rebuild their relationships. Opening with worship or a Scripture meditation can be a part of this. Joining in prayer and worship and reflecting on passages of Scripture are the activities from which all theological discussion arises.

Very few people instantly understand something they read. In typical groups, after reading a short paper or article aloud, it is useful to offer a brief minute or two of silent reflection, and ask participants to identify two or three elements that interested or puzzled them. The first rounds of conversation often have the function of clarifying what the paper or article is saying. Later rounds of conversation move into reflection, implications, and application. Focus questions are often helpful here.

If you are responsible for leading a group, it will be important to read the essays in a section beforehand and assess where you think your group can best begin. What short piece might be most accessible? What aspects of the issue would most likely engage their interest? Consider the literacy levels in your group. It may be best to read the paper aloud and stop frequently to let people reflect and ask questions.

SOME SUGGESTED PROCESS MODELS

+ You might begin with one of the short papers — reading it aloud and taking time together to discuss and respond to it. The Reflection following most of the papers suggests lines of inquiry that people may wish to follow.

+ You might start with one of the short dialogues, reading it aloud with different group members each assigned to one of the voices. Then you might canvass group members about which of the perspectives they felt most in sympathy with, and which they found offered them the greatest challenges. The next step might be reading the paper that precedes the dialogue.

◆ Group members may follow up the brief information presented in one or more of the boxes, perhaps finding a piece of the writing by one of the writers mentioned in a box and presenting it at a follow-up session. Or they may look up further information on a theme or idea briefly explained in one of the boxes and present that at a follow-up session.

◆ As part of an ongoing Christian education strategy in a congregation, any of the short papers might be copied and used as an insert in a parish newsletter or service leaflet. It could also serve as the subject of a sermon.

◆ As part of a program of mission, group members might consider how the issues addressed in this book might be perceived by someone who is just beginning to inquire about the Christian faith. Members of the group can imagine themselves to be people who have just walked into a Christian setting for the first time in their lives. What questions come to their minds? List the questions on a board or flip chart and try to answer them.

◆ Here is a strategy to encourage everyone to participate in discussion: Going around the group, and starting at the beginning of one of the statements, each person reads a few lines or a paragraph until the whole statement has been read. Then, going around the group again, each person offers some response — a question, a reflection, a statement, a personal anecdote. It may be useful to set a time limit on responses of a minute or two. No one interrupts to question or comment on anyone else's response until all responses have been heard. Further general discussion may follow.

◆ Here is another exercise that the Commission found fruitful: Identify a major topic of theology such as sin, grace, salvation, authority, creation, redemption, etc. Give the group members one sheet of paper and ask them to write what our faith has to say about the topic in no more than 200 words. (This could be done in about 20 minutes of the group's time, or as an exercise prior to a session.) Then read aloud to one another your 200-word statements. Consider together: How are they similar? How do they diverge in approach or emphasis? This exercise will build members' skill in stating aspects of faith clearly and succinctly, and could be a good exercise in equipping a group preparing for intentional evangelism with seekers.

THE PARISH OF RUSSELL (DIOCESE OF OTTAWA) DISCUSSION PROCESS

This process was designed for a group meeting for 90 minutes, with a firm commitment to stop after 90 minutes have expired. The discussion focuses on a different excerpt or "article" in each session. Before each session assign to different group members one of three tasks:

1. Ask one group member to read the article for the next session beforehand, and come prepared to open the session with a short Bible reading that she or he thinks relates to or responds to the article.

2. Ask one or two group members to prepare to read the article aloud when the group meets.

3. Ask one group member to read the article for the next session beforehand, and write a short prayer for use to close the discussion session.

When the group meets:

Step 1. Begin the meeting with a short Bible reading.

Step 2. Read the selected article aloud. After finishing, take two minutes of silence for reflection. Reading aloud and the silence are an important part of what makes this process work well.

Step 3. First go-round of discussion. In this go-round, every member has an opportunity to speak once for as long as they wish in response to the article. When each member has finished, if another wishes to comment, they must first ask permission of the one who has just spoken. That individual has the right to say, "Yes," "No," or "I'd prefer to wait."

Step 4. After all have had an opportunity to speak once, then the floor is open for any and all to discuss freely.

Step 5. Five minutes before the contracted time is up, take a couple of minutes in silence to gather thoughts; then pray together the prayer prepared by the group member beforehand.

ROBERT CROUSE, Ph.D., D.D., is a priest of the Diocese of Nova Scotia and Bishop Short Canon Theologian, Diocese of Saskatchewan. His current appointments include: Professor Emeritus of Classics, Dalhousie University, and the University of King's College, Halifax, Nova Scotia; Adjunct Professor of Theology, Trinity Episcopal School for Ministry, Ambridge, PA., USA; Adjunct Professor of Classics, Dalhousie University; Visiting Professor of Patrology, Augustinian Patristic Institute, Pontifical Lateran University, Rome; Honorary President, Prayer Book Society of Canada. He speaks at many national and international conferences and is the author of numerous essays, articles, and published sermons, many available at www.3.ns.sympatico.ca/angelweb/rdc2.htm (includes cv and bibliography).

EDITH MARY HUMPHREY received her doctorate in 1991 from McGill University, specializing in New Testament and early Christian origins, and was awarded the Governor General's Gold Medal for excellence. She is a frequent speaker for conferences and retreats, and has lectured in Hebrew Bible and New Testament at McGill (Montreal), Wycliffe College (Toronto), Bishop's University (Lennoxville), Regent College (Vancouver) Tyndale Seminary (Toronto and Ottawa), and various universities in Ottawa. She is the author of a guide to the ancient romance *Joseph and Aseneth* (Sheffield, June, 2000), and the monograph *The Ladies and the Cities: Transformation and Apocalyptic Identity in Joseph and Aseneth, 4 Ezra, the Apocalypse and The Shepherd of Hermas*

(JSPS 17; Sheffield, 1995), as well as various articles on rhetoric and visionary literature. Her popular writing tackles various contemporary issues in the church, and includes the Dare booklet *A Solid Foundation? — The Seven Pillars of the Jesus Seminar Re-examined.* Currently she is writing a popular book on Christian spirituality, a short preview of which appears in the April edition of *Christianity Today*, entitled "It's Not About Us."

Edith was a Salvation Army officer with her husband, Christopher, for five years, joined the Anglican Communion in 1984, and currently serves as musical director of St. George's Church (Ottawa), where she is a member with Chris and her three daughters. She is an executive member of both the Canadian Society of Biblical Studies and the Canadian Evangelical Theological Association. She has served on the Primate's Theological Commission (ACC) and the theological commission for the Diocese of New Westminster, and is Professor of Scripture at Augustine College (Ottawa).

WALTER W.G. DELLER, B.Mus., M.Div., Th.D, is the Principal and Professor of Old Testament and Congregational Life at the College of Emmanuel and St. Chad in Saskatoon, Saskatchewan. After musical studies at Brandon University and working as a community musician in Nova Scotia, he studied theology at Trinity College, Toronto School of Theology. His doctoral dissertation in Old Testament, *Tehillim: The Rhetoric of Ensemble*, looked at the shaping and reader reception of the book of Psalms. After a short period of work at Henry Budd College for

Ministry in The Pas, Manitoba, he returned to Toronto, where for ten years he was a member of the diocesan Program Resources staff, first as Coordinator of the LOGOS Institute, and then as Director of Program Resources. His professional work has included Bible study training events, clergy conferences, adult education curriculum development, work with congregations in the areas of planning and conflict, and consulting in the area of change in complex systems. For almost twenty years he was the assistant organist in the parish of St. Martin-in-the-Fields in West Toronto. From 1998 he acted as educational consultant to the Primate's Theological Commission, and since 2001 has been a member of the commission.

LAVERNE JACOBS, B.A., M.Div. The Rev. Canon Laverne Jacobs is a graduate of the University of Windsor and Huron College. He is in a shared ministry serving the Church of St. John the Baptist (Anglican) and the Walpole Island United Church, Walpole Island, Ontario. Laverne is Ojibwe from the Walpole Island First Nation. He was ordained to the priesthood in 1975 and served at Walpole Island and Forest/Kettle Point in the Diocese of Huron before joining General Synod staff as the Coordinator for Native Ministries from 1987–1996. As a First Nations priest, Laverne has had to wrestle with what it means to be Native and Christian and in the process debunk internalized messages from the church that called his heritage into question. He is committed to advocating for justice and self-determination for First Nations people. He

and his wife, Lynn, have three children and seven grandchildren.

HANNA KASSIS was born in Gaza, Palestine, where he was baptized in the Episcopal Church. He received his elementary and secondary education at the Bishop Gobat School in Jerusalem. After a stint as a school teacher and "house father" at the Lutheran School for Orphans in Bethlehem, he began his studies in 1956 in Near Eastern archaeology at the American University of Beirut, Lebanon (BA 1959). He studied Near Eastern languages and archaeology at Harvard University (1960–1964; Ph.D. 1965). From 1964 until his retirement in 1997 he taught Biblical Studies, Near Eastern Archaeology and Islamic Studies at the University of British Columbia. He is currently a recurring Visiting Professor of Medieval Studies at the Central European University in Budapest, Hungary, teaching courses on Christian-Muslim-Jewish relations in the Middle Ages.

His publications include a *Concordance of the Qur'an*, which has opened the text of the sacred book of Islam to many who do not have a mastery of its language.

CHRISTOPHER LIND, Ph.D., traces his spiritual formation to the junior choir of St. Jude's, Oakville, Ontario. As a theological student he was nurtured by the Church of the Holy Trinity, Toronto. He is presently a member of the congregation of St. John's Cathedral, Saskatoon. He holds degrees from York University, Trinity College, and St. Michael's College, all in Toronto.

From 1985 to 1998 he served as Professor of Church and Society at St. Andrew's College, Saskatoon, and currently he is President of St. Andrew's College and St. Stephen's College, sponsored by the United Church of Canada. A lay person, he writes on ethics and economics, contextual theology, and practical ethics. He is the author of *Something's Wrong Somewhere: Globalization, Community and the Moral Economy of the Farm Crisis*, and the co-editor of *Coalitions for Justice: Canada's Interchurch Coalitions*, as well as *Justice as Mission: An Agenda for the Church*.

VICTORIA MATTHEWS, B.A., M.Div., Th.M., has been Bishop of Edmonton since 1997. She was ordained to the diaconate, priesthood, and episcopate in the Diocese of Toronto, where she served in rural and suburban parishes and as the Area Bishop of the Credit Valley, and also part-time at Trinity College, Toronto, as Director of Field Placements and Tutor in pastoral theology. Her interests in theology include particularly the Oxford Movement and Patristics. She served as a member of the Design Group for the 1998 Lambeth Conference and as a member of the Communication Task Force during the Conference. She is also a member of the Corporation of Yale University. In the Anglican Church of Canada she has served on National Executive Council, Doctrine and Worship Committee and the Book of Alternative Services Evaluation Commission. Victoria was appointed Chairperson of the Primate's Theological Commission in 1996.

JOANNE ELIZABETH McWILLIAM, M.A., Ph.D., is a priest of the Diocese of Toronto, Honorary Assistant at Christ Church, Deer Park, and professor emeritus of the University of Toronto and Trinity College, Toronto. She is a graduate of Loretto Abbey, St. Michael's College, and the University of Toronto. She has also taught at the University of Detroit and The General Theological Seminary, New York City. She is author of two books, *The Theology of Grace of Theodore of Mopsuestia,* and *Death and Resurrection in the Fathers,* and many articles, and editor of *Augustine: Rhetor to Theologian.* Currently she is working on a book on Augustine's christology. She is also member and past president of The Canadian Society for Patristic Studies, The Canadian Theological Society, and The American Theological Society. Married to the Rev. C. Peter Slater, she has, by a previous marriage, four children, and twelve grandchildren.

MICHAEL GEOFFREY PEERS is Primate of the Anglican Church of Canada. He has an interpreter's certificate for German-English translation from the University of Heidelberg (1955), a Bachelor of Arts in Slavic Studies from the University of British Columbia (1956), and a Licentiate in Theology from Trinity College, Toronto (1959). He has received numerous honorary degrees over the years, including a doctorate in 1988 from the University of Kent (Canterbury).

He was ordained as a priest in the Diocese of Ottawa in 1960, and has served the Anglican

Church as university chaplain (Ottawa, 1961–1966), parish priest (Winnipeg, 1966-1974), Dean of Qu'Appelle (Regina, 1974–1977), Bishop of the Diocese of Qu'Appelle (1977–1986), and Metropolitan of the Province of Rupert's Land (1982–1986). He was elected to the office of Primate by the 31st General Synod held in Winnipeg in 1986.

As Primate, Michael Peers is especially concerned to encourage greater inclusiveness in the life of the church, and to address major issues facing Canada and the world from a Christian perspective. By virtue of his position, he is also President of the Metropolitan Council of Cuba, providing a personal link between the Cuban Episcopal Church and the rest of the Anglican Communion. He is fluent in French, German, and Russian, as well as English. He is known as a strong supporter of ecumenism and, since 1991, has served on the Central Committee of the World Council of Churches.

Michael Peers is married to Dorothy Elizabeth (Bradley); they have three grown children.

DAVID A. REED, M.A, Ph.D., a priest of the Diocese of Toronto, is Honorary Assistant at St. Paul's L'Amoreaux, Scarborough. He was reared as a Pentecostal in New Brunswick, and eventually became one of four brothers to enter ordained ministry. After a brief teaching career at New Brunswick Institute of Technology, he moved to New England to study theology. While there he became an Episcopalian, was ordained and pastored for 18 years in Massachusetts and Connecticut. He completed his Ph.D. in System-

atic Theology at Boston University. His thesis is still the fundamental work on Oneness Pentecostalism, the third and heterodox stream of the modern Pentecostal movement. Since 1987 he has been professor of pastoral theology and Director of Field Education at Wycliffe College, Toronto. He continues to pursue interest in pastoral theology, contextual education, Pentecostal-charismatic theology, and spiritual movements in the church and culture, including cults. His publications have appeared in magazines, journals, books, and dictionaries. He is currently writing a book on Oneness Pentecostalism. His wife, Carlynn, deserves credit for stimulating his ongoing interest in marriage and family studies. He also enjoys being a "techie" for her theatrical productions. They have two sons, Kirk and Chris, and live in Unionville.

EILEEN SCULLY, Ph.D., is a cradle Anglican who, like many of her generation, left the Anglican Church, in her case for some "ecumenical wandering" in her late teens and twenties, returning home in the early 1990s. That ecumenical wandering led her to studies in Systematic and Historical Theology at St. Michael's College, Toronto (Roman Catholic), and pastoral studies at Waterloo Lutheran Seminary. She is the "junior" member of the Commission, having been born well after the baby-boom. She teaches on a part-time basis at Thorneloe University, Huron College, and Renison College, otherwise known as the "Ontario Anglican Circuit Preacher Route of Sessional Lecturers." Eileen worked for five years staffing ecumenical theological dialogues at the Canadian Council of Churches. Her theological work has been in the area of theology of grace, theological methodology, ecclesiology, and questions of Anglican identity. Her perspective has been shaped by a number of different experiences and relationships: "classical" training in historical theology, pastoral theology, feminist and other liberationist perspectives, ecumenical dialogues and, most recently, partnership with First Nations peoples. She is married to Eric Duerrstein, and they live in Waterloo, Ontario, with their two young sons, Michael and Colin, who are the real theologians in the family.

Bibliography

Bede, the Venerable. *History of the English Church and People*. Harmondsworth: Penguin, 1968.

Bunyan, John. *The Pilgrim's Progress*. London: A. and C. Black, 1904.

Calvin, Jean. *The Institutes of the Christian Religion* [1509-64]. John T. McNeil, ed. Translation by Ford Lewis Battle. Philadelphia: Westminister, 1960.

Catechism of the Catholic Church. Rome. Vatican City, 1992.

Celebrating Common Prayer. London: Mowbray, 1992.

Cranmer, Thomas. *On the True and Catholic Doctrine of the Lord's Supper*. C.H.H. Wright, ed. London: C.J. Thynne, 1907.

Crockett, William. *Eucharist:Symbol of Transformatin*. New York: Pueblo Publishing Company, 1989.

DiNoia, J.A. "Karl Rahner", *The Modern Theologians,* ed. David Ford. Oxford: Blackwells, 1997.

Fox, Matthew. *Original Blessing*. Santa Fe, New Mexico: Bear and Co., 1983.

Hobart, John Henry. *A Companion to the Book of Common Prayer* [1805]. New York: Swords, Stanford, 1827.

Hooker, Richard. *Treatise on the Laws of Ecclesiastical Polity* [1594–97]. New York: Everyman's Library, 1907–65.

James, William. *The Varieties of Religious Experience*. London: Longmans, Green and Co., 1911.

Jewel, John. *An Apology of the Church of England* [1564]. J.E. Booty, ed. Ithaca: Cornell University Press. Printed for the Folger Shakespeare Library, 1963.

_____. *Reply to Harding*. in *Works*. J. Ayre, ed. 4 vols. London: Parker Society, 1845–50.

Kempis, Thomas à. *The Imitation of Christ* [1418]. Translation L. Sherley-Price. Harmondsworth: Penguin Classics, 1962.

Kierkegaard, Soren. *Fear and Trembling*. Translation with introduction, Walter Lowrie. New York: Doubleday Anchor, 1954.

_____. *Philosophical Fragments*. Translation David F. Swenson. Princeton, NJ: Princeton University Press, 1936.

_____. *Edifying Discourses*. Translation David F. and Lilian Marvin Swenson. Augsburg Press, 1941–48.

Kirk, Kenneth. *The Vision of God*. London: Longmans, Green, 1931.

Lame Deer, John. *Meditations with Native Americans—Lakota Spirituality.* Santa Fe, New Mexico: Bear and Co., 1984.

Law, William. *A Serious Call to a Devout and Holy Life.* New York/Mahwah: Paulist Press, 1978.

Price, Charles P. and Louis Weil. *Liturgy for Living.* New York: Seabury, 1979.

Reynolds, Edward. *Meditations on the Holy Sacraments* in *Works,* 6 vols. London: T. Newcomb, 1679.

Sedgwick, Timothy. *The Christian Moral Life.* Grand Rapids: Eerdmans, 1999.

Sider, Ron. *Rich Christians in a World of Hunger.* Downer's Grove, Illinois: Inter-Varsity Press, 1984.

Stevenson, Robert Louis. *A Christmas Sermon.* Toronto: Musson, 1888.

Stott, John. *Christian Mission in the Modern World.* London: Falcon, 1975.

_____. *Involvement: Being a Responsible Christian in a Non-Christian Society.* Old Tappan, NJ: F.H. Reynolds Co.,1985.

Temple, Frederick. *The Relations between Religion and Science* [The Bampton Lectures, 1884]. London: Macmillan, 1884.

Tillich, Paul. *Systematic Theology.* 3 vols. Chicago: University of Chicago, 1956–63.

_____. *The Courage to Be.* New Haven: Yale University Press, 1952.

Tozer, A.W. *The Pursuit of God.* Harrisburg, Pennsylvania: Christian Publications Inc., 1948.

Underhill, Evelyn. *Mysticism: a Study in the Nature and Development of Man's Spiritual Consciousness.* 17th edition. London: Methuen, 1949.

Wilkinson, John. *Egeria's Travels.* London: SPCK, 1971.

World Council of Churches. *Baptism, Eucharist and Ministry.* Faith and Order Papers #111, 1982.

Wright, J. Robert. *Prayer Book Spirituality.* New York: CHC, 1989.

Index of Explanatory Notes